GREAT PASS UNDER HEAVEN

摄影　王　金
撰文　胡　杨

甘肃人民美术出版社

前　言

祁连山的支脉文殊山连绵起伏；马鬃山的支脉黑山，如怒如涛。在这两山之间宽约15公里的平坦峡谷，地势险要，是千里河西走廊最狭窄的地段之一，也是东西交通的唯一孔道，古称为“河西第一隘口”。明长城西端的起点、“天下第一雄关”——嘉峪关就修建在这条峡谷的山岗上。

嘉峪关是一个庞大的建筑物。关城层楼重叠，飞檐凌空，巍峨宏伟，气势壮观。关城两翼，坚固的长城爬山越岭，蜿蜒逶迤，烽墩众多，布局合理，形成了一个壁垒森严的军事防御体系。作为主建筑，关城的设计十分考究。它由内城、瓮城、外城、楼阁和附属建筑组成，重城并守，易守难攻。内城城高9米，周长640米，面积25000平方米，城墙用黄土夯筑和土坯垒筑而成，西宽东窄，略呈梯形。城墙上部两侧建有1.7米高的砖砌垛墙，外墙设有垛口，形如碉堡。远望，高墙纵横，城堞林立，气壮山河；近观，雕梁画栋，色彩艳丽，建筑精湛。“磨砖砌就鱼鳞瓦，五彩装成碧玉楼”，作为长城遗址中规模最大、保存最完整的军事防御体系，嘉峪关已被列为国家级重点文物保护单位，被列入世界文化遗产。

据记载，嘉峪关一带早有设防。汉代设玉石障，曾派兵镇守。五代时黑山脚下设有天门关。明洪武五年（公元1372年），征虏大将军冯胜驻兵河西，他看中了嘉峪山麓这块咽喉之地，在这里首筑土城。

当地的老百姓流传着这样一句格言：“先有嘉峪关，后有明长城”，表达了人们自豪的心情，史实也是的确如此。筑于明朝初年的嘉峪关，至今已有六百多岁，它与山海关遥遥相对，都有“天下第一关”之称，但嘉峪关年代更早，历史更悠久。

雄关如铁，长城主宰，巍然屹立的嘉峪关，不愧是河西走廊的一颗明珠，不愧为中国长城的瑰宝。

Preface

The Wenshu Mountain, a branch of the Qilian Mountains, winds endlessly. The Black mountain, a branch of the Mazong Mouatains, bowls with waves. Between them, is an even valley with the width of about 15 kilometers. Here is one of the narrowest places of the Thousand-Li-Hexi-Corridor. The surrounding terrain is strategically situated. The valley is also the only path for east-west transportation, which was called "the First Mountain Pass in Hexi" in history. Jiayu Pass, "The Greatest Pass under Heaven", the western beginning of the Ming Great Wall, was built on a hill of this valley.

Jiayu Pass is a huge building. With storeys above storeys, flying eaves high in the air, the castle is towering and grand. In the two sides of the Pass, the solid Great Wall winds its way through the mountains. With many platforms, they form a strongly fortified military defense system. As the main building, the castle was designed very carefully. It is composed of the inner city, the court city, the outer city, towers and annexes. With city after city, it is easy to defend and difficult to attack. With a height of 9 meters, a perimeter of 640 meters and an area of 25000 square meters, the inner city is trapezoid, being wider in the west and narrower in the east. The wall was built with yellow earth and earth bricks. On it, the battlements are like pillboxes with walls of 17 meters high. From far, high walls criss-cross, from near, beams carved and rafters painted colourfully. As a military defense system, being largest and intact in the Great Wall relics, Jiayu Pass was listed as one of the important preserved cultural relic unit of the nation, and as one of cultural relics of the world.

目　录 Contents

嘉峪关市旅游景点示意图

悬壁长城

黑山石刻

魏晋墓画像砖

世纪龙林

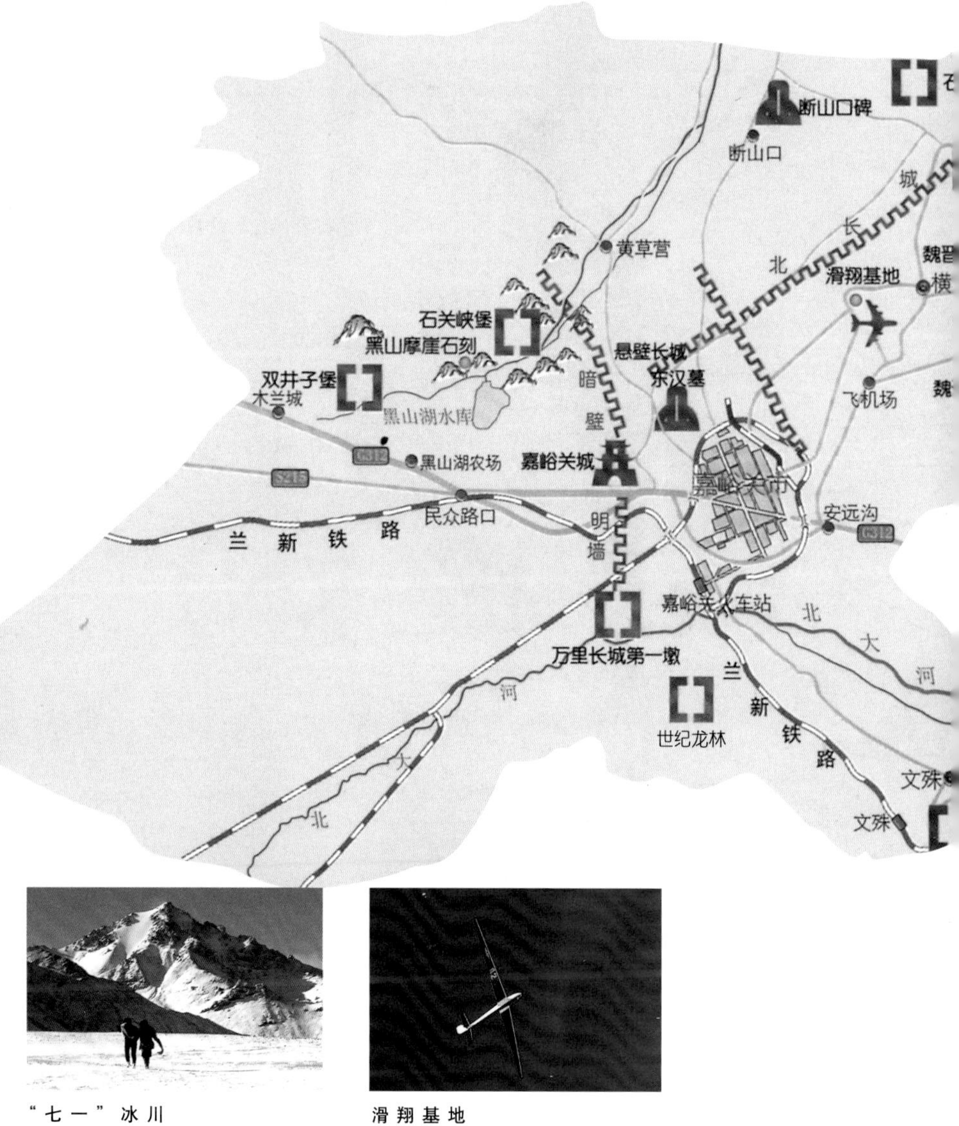

长城第一墩

“七一”冰川

滑翔基地

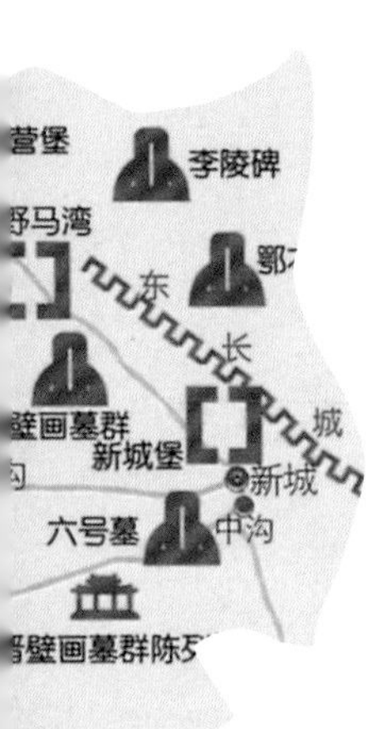

选 址 建 关 Selecting the Location to Build the Pass

嘉峪关在明代是甘肃镇肃州卫的前哨，是西北的防务要地。它北依马鬃山，南据祁连山，两山夹峙之间，只有一条宽十多公里的通道，古称“河西第一隘口”。那么当初是什么人慧眼识聪，在这里选址建关呢？

据说是明朝洪武年间，朱元璋派征虏大将军冯胜，追歼元朝的残兵败将。冯胜大将军率兵西进，直取河西走廊。他雄勇多智，大破元兵于甘州（今张掖）一带，进军肃州（今酒泉）直达居延海、玉门关外，所向无敌，连连报捷，收复河西，建立奇功。朱元璋为了巩固西北边陲，命他在河西建关设防。

冯胜大将军遵照旨意，带领众将，骑马日行夜宿，仔细观察这一带的地形。原来这号称“走廊”的地带，很多地方宽度大都在一二百里开外，防守困难，很难找到适合建关的地方。

有一天，冯胜将军骑马来到肃州西面五十里的嘉峪山下，见这里祁连山雄峙于南，马鬃山耸立于北，西接群山大漠，东连平畴绿野，依山靠水，地势险要，这才是建关的好地方呀！冯胜大将军率领众将领，骑马涉过冬夏澄清的“九眼泉”，登上嘉峪山，仔细观看了山形水势，情不自禁地赞叹：“此乃咽喉之地，地势天成，妙啊！”他又看看脚下，山势平坦，基石牢固，方圆有五十亩地开外，真是建关设防的好地方。众将领也异口同声地说：“这里狭谷似瓶，易守难攻，修建关口，定然固若金汤！”他便与众将商议，决定在此建关。

冯将军就将关址选定在此处，立即破土动工，不到一年，就修筑了周长二百二十丈的嘉峪雄关。

Jiayu Pass was the outpost of Suzhouwei in Gansu town and the very important defense place in the Northwest in the Ming Dynasty. It is situated at the foot of Mazong Mountain in the North, with Qilian Mountain lying in the South. Cutting between the two mountains, there is a passage with width of only more than 10 kilometers, which was called "the First Mountain Pass in the West River" in history. Then, who was the clear-sighted to choose this place to build the Pass?

It is said that during the years of Hongwu in the Ming Dynasty, the Conquest General Fengsheng was sent to pursue and wipe out the remnants of the army of Yuan Dynasty. With good news in succession, he reoccupied the West River area. To consolidate the frontier in the Northwest, Zhuyuanzhang ordered him to build Passes and guards in the West River. The Great General Fengsheng obeyed his instruction, rode by horse with his generals day after day to conspect the topography carefully.

Some day, Fengsheng rode to the foot of Jiayu Mountain, which was 50 Lis in the west of Suzhou. With Qilian Mountain Lying greatly in the South, Mazong Mountain standing highly in the North, joining with mountains and the great desert in the west and connecting to the level fields and the greens in the east, at the foot of a hill and beside a stream, with the surrounding terrain strategically situated and difficult of access, this is just the good place to build the pass! The other generals all agreed that. "The valley here is like a bottle, easy to defend and difficult to attack. A pass built here must be as strong as iron." So they decided to build the pass here.

The General Feng chose the pass location here, broke ground at once. In less than one year, the great Jiayu Pass had been built with the perimeter of 220 Zhangs.

一 块 砖

A Brick

登上嘉峪关城楼，在柔远楼西侧的城台，可见一块古代的青砖，安放在西瓮城阁楼的后檐台上。人们说，这块古砖是一块定城砖。

传说明朝正德元年，在修建嘉峪关时，有位工匠师傅，名叫易开占，不仅技术高超，而且善于设计和计算，胜似鲁班，声望很高。接受了修建嘉峪关的工程之后，易师傅和众工匠齐心协力，不仅制定出了布局精巧、结构坚固的设计方案，还精确地计算出用料数量。当他把设计方案和用料计划交给负责承修的监官时，这个贪心糊涂的监官，根本不相信眼前这个土模土样的工匠会有如此神算，便逼问易师傅：“你计算的真有这么精确？”易师傅哈哈一笑，答道：“没有错，错了我受罚。”

负责承修工程的监官，就按易师傅的方案备料，故意多加了一块砖。易师傅和众工匠按照设计精心施工，计划用料。经过无数个昼夜的辛勤劳作，终于使楼阁凌空、气势雄壮的关城巍然屹立于戈壁大漠之中。

然而对于多出的一块砖，众工匠心里却捏着一把汗，只有易师傅不慌不忙地把它放置于西瓮城阁楼上。当监官大呼小叫：“易开占，你怎么多出了一块砖？明日午时三刻便是你的断魂时。”易师傅大喊：“住手！那是一块定城砖，要是搬掉，全城立时就要倒塌。”监官听了，灰溜溜地走了。

Climbing up the Jiayu Pass castle, on the platform of the west side of Rou Yuan Tower, you can see a historic brick placed at the rear eaves of the attic of the West Court City. People say this is a brick to stabilize the castle. A legend says there was a reputed craftsman named Yi Kaizhan. After having accepted the project of Jiayu Pass, Master Yi and his men not only made out ingenious designing plan but also exactly calculated out the quantity of materials. When he hand it to the supervisor, this greedy & foolish officer did not believe the bumpkin-looking craftsman and asked him with threatening tone “Is your calculation really so exact?”. Master Yi laughed: “Yes, otherwise I accept punishment”.

The supervisor purposely added one brick according to Master Yi’s calculation. Master Yi and his men constructed the Pass according to his design & plan. Finally a pompous castle with pavilions high up in the air stood towering in the dessert after hard work.

As other craftsmen were worrying about the extra brick, Master Yi put it to the attic of the West Court City. When the supervisor shouted: “Yi Kaizhan, why there is a brick extra? You’ll be killed tomorrow lunch time.” And Master Yi shouted back: “Stop, this is a brick to stable the castle. If removed, the whole city would collapse at once”. Hearing this, the officer went away gloomily.

高楼从顶建

Building the Tower From the Top

嘉峪关的"光化门"和"柔远门"，9米高的方形平台之上，都建有高达17米的楼阁。

俗话说："高楼万丈平地起。"可是，这两座城楼，却是从楼顶往下建的。

传说大明正德元年八月中秋，肃州兵备副宪李端澄奉命修建嘉峪关城的东、西二楼，他委托肃州卫嘉峪关承信校尉王镇承办这项工程。

王镇领受了任务以后，反复琢磨：要在三丈来高的土筑城台上修建五丈多高的大楼，不是一件容易的事。于是，乘中秋佳节，他邀请了附近知名的工匠，在关城城台之上，边赏月边商议这件事，让大家出点子，想计谋。众工匠你一言我一语，出了不少主意，王镇听了之后，连连摇头。这时，有一位平时寡言少语的老工匠开了腔："这么高的楼阁，还是要从顶建。"王镇一怔，当老工匠慢条斯理地说出了他的全部想法之后，众工匠连连点头称赞，认为这是个好法子。大家又作了一些补充，作出了这样一套完整的施工方案：先在楼台之上，堆起土盖楼顶，然后竖立三楼的立柱。把三楼建成后，将土刨掉，再建二层楼。二层建毕，刨掉二层的土，最后修建最底层。

工匠们认真备料，细心施工。楼阁从顶上一层又一层地修建，土一层又一层地刨出，到了来年二月，关城之上东、西两座雄伟的高楼便顺利建成了。

The Towers "Guanghuamen" and "Rouyuanmen" of Jiayu Pass were both built on the square platform of 9 meters high, and both with pavilions of 17 meters high.

These two city towers were built from the top downward.

It is said that at the Mid-autumn of the first year of Zhende in the Ming Dynasty, the officer Wang Zhen was entrusted to undertake the project.

Wang Zhen accepted the task and thought it over: it's not easy to build a 5-zhang -high tower on the 3-zhang-high earth-built platform. By taking the opportunity of the Festival, he invited the known craftsmen nearby to discuss about it while enjoying the full moon on the platform. The craftsmen presented their own ideas and Wang Zhen could not accept one. Then a silent old craftsman said:"we should build such a high pavilion from the top." Wang Zhen was shocked and then praised the plan with other craftsmen after the craftsman brought out all his idea slowly. Then they made out a complete construction plan: on the platform, heap earth high enough to build the tower top, then build the third storey. After that dig away some earth to build the second storey, and then the first storey and the bottom.

The craftsmen carefully made the preparations and built the pavilions from the top. In February of the next year, the majestic East &West towers in the Pass were finished.

冰 道 运 石

Transporting Stones on the Ice Road

当人们走进嘉峪关城，就会看见楼阁台阶、城墙基础和门洞铺设的无数的巨型石条。这些长约二米，宽五十厘米，厚三十厘米的青石石条，是从哪里来的呢？又是怎样运到嘉峪关关城的呢？

据说，在当初建关城时，因需要大量的石条，供施工用，石匠们就四处寻找，经过察看，终于在关西北十多公里处的黑山中一个叫磨子沟的地方找到了这种石头。那里盛产地溜石，石质坚硬，可凿成磨盘、碾磙等物。石匠们取了样品，经鉴定，确定用磨子沟的石头做基石。于是，石匠们到磨子沟开采石条。石条凿成之后，人抬不起，路程又远，运输十分困难。工匠们边凿石条边犯愁，眼看隆冬季节到了，石条还没运出山，工期又催得很紧，怎么办呢？

这时候，有位老石匠开了腔：“我看，顺山坡修一条路吧，冬季一到，就在路上泼水，结冰以后，往下滑，看这样行不行？”大伙一听，都说这是一个好办法。禀告监工，得到批准后，就开始修路。滴水成冰的季节一到，便调动车辆人夫，拉水、担水，往路面上一泼，水很快凝结成冰，一条冰道出现在山间。人们站到冰道两边，手持撬杠使巨大的石条沿冰道向山下滑行，然后用牛车拉。工匠们就用这办法把所有的石条一块接一块，运到了关城的工地上，保证了关城的工程按期完工。

Entering Jiayu Pass, you will see numerous huge stone plates paved on the steps, in the base of the wall and the gates. The stone plates are of 2 m long, 50 cm wide and 30 cm thick. Where did they come from? And how were they transported to Jiayu Pass?

It' s said that a large number of stone plates were needed when building the Pass, the stone craftsmen looked for them everywhere and finally found the stone at a place named Mozigou in the Black Mountain over 10 km north-west of the Pass. After appraisement, the stone craftsmen decided to use them for the base. But when the stones were made, they were too heavy for people to carry. As winter was drawing near, how could the craftsmen transport the stone plates within such a tight schedule?

Then an old stone-man began to speak:“in my opinion, build a road along the slope, when winter comes, we splash water onto the road, slide down the stone plates after the water is frozen, is it OK?”. Everybody thought it was a good idea. Then they began to build a road. When the cold winter came, they splashed water onto the road and soon an ice road came into being. Standing at both sides of the road, people slid down the huge plates along the road by crowbars and then transported them by oxcart. In this way, they transported all stone plates to the jobsite and this guaranteed the schedule.

山 羊 驮 砖

The Goat Carrying Bricks on the Back

嘉峪关作为长城沿线规模最大的军事防御体系，其用砖的数量十分惊人。据说，当时修建关城所用的砖，是在关西四十里以外的地方烧制的。砖烧好以后，用牛车拉到关城下，然后再一块一块背上城墙。这种办法速度很慢，眼看有贻误工期的危险，人们都焦急万分。

有一天，有一个放羊娃赶着一群山羊，在关城附近放牧。他看见人们弯腰驼砖，个个筋疲力尽，监工还在不停的吆喝着，他心情十分沉重。怎么能够帮助人们摆脱这繁重的劳役呢？憨厚的孩子在斜坡马道上来回走动，想着想着，他突然高兴地喊道："有办法啦！"

他甩着响鞭，吆喝着把羊赶到了城下，解下腰带，一头拴一块砖，搭在羊背上。他用手轻轻一拍羊屁股，只见身体轻巧的山羊驮着砖，"噔噔噔"一溜小跑爬上了又高又陡的城墙。背砖的人们看了喜出望外。

这时候，只见放羊娃站在城头，一声唿哨，一群群山羊从四面八方拥到关城下。人们解下腰带，拴好砖，驱赶着一群又一群山羊，驮着砖从马道登上高高的城墙。

As a largest-scale defense system along the Great Wall, Jiayu Pass used a very surprisely large quantity of bricks. It's said the bricks for the Pass were baked 40 miles west of the Pass, then they were carried to site by oxcart and shouldered to the wall. It was not effective and people worried about the schedule.

One day, a child goatherd was driving a horde of goats grazing near the Pass. He saw people hunchbacked to carry bricks and exhausted, the supervisors were berating. The child was very sad. How could people get rid of the strenuous work? Thinking over & over the child suddenly shouted out:"I have an idea!"

Cracking his whip, he drove the goats to the foot of the castle, unfastened the belt and tied a brick on each end of the belt and then put it on the back of a goat, he gently patted the goat's end, and the goat climbed up the steep wall with ease. Seeing this, the people carrying bricks were overjoyed.

At the moment, people saw the child standing in the front of the castle, with a whistle, hordes of goats crowded at the foot of the castle. Then people followed suit and saved efforts.

在嘉峪关关城正门两侧和内城门北侧，如果用两块石头相击，就可以隐隐听到"啾啾"的燕鸣声，这其中，有一段凄凉而美丽的传说。

在明朝正德年间，有两只燕子筑巢于嘉峪关城内。每天黎明，两只燕子相伴飞出关城觅食；傍晚，夜幕降临，又双双飞回关内巢中歇息。它们朝夕生活在一起，形影不离。

一天清早，同往常一样，两只燕子又一同飞出关外觅食。当夕阳西下之时，雌燕在前，雄燕在后，两只燕子高高兴兴飞向关内。不料，当雌燕飞进关城后的一刹那，突然狂风大作，飞沙走石，天昏地暗，什么也看不清楚。雄燕被卷在风沙中然迷失了方向。当雄燕好不容易找到关城时，关门已经紧闭，不能入关。雄燕心急如焚，情急之下，竟一头向城门撞去……

雌燕久等雄燕不归，悲痛欲绝，便不时发出"啾啾"之声。人们说那是雌燕不死的灵魂。

也有人说，西出嘉峪关，一路戈壁，前途凶险，只要在这里敲击石头，能听见燕子鸣叫的声音，就可平安归来。

击 石 燕 鸣

A Swallow Sings When Striking the Stone

At both sides of the main entrance and northern side of the inner city, if you strike one stone with another, you will hear the faint "jug, jug" of swallows, it is a sad &beautiful legend.

During the year of Zhengde in the Ming Dynasty, two swallows nested their home inside the city of Jiayu Pass. They hunted food in company at every sunrise and flied back to the nest together at every dusk. They lived together closely.

One morning, as usual, the two swallows flied out for hunting food. At sun fall, they were merrily flying to the inside Pass. As soon as the female one flew into the city gate, suddenly there was a blustering gale, the world was in a chaos and darkness, and the male swallow lost his way. When he found the Pass gate, it was tightly closed. The male swallow was so impatient and bumped his head to the city gate in an impulse.

The female swallow waited & waited, but the male swallow never came back. She was so heart-stricken and made the "jug, jug" at times. And people say that is the undying soul of the female swallow.

九 眼 泉 Nine-eye Spring

嘉峪关下有九眼泉，泉水冬夏澄清，碧波不竭，景色秀丽。

相传，当年修建嘉峪关时，数万名民夫汇集一处，腾起滚滚烟尘，一时间，饮水成了最大的问题。没有水，延误了修筑长城的工期，可不是闹着玩的。于是官府又抽调大量的民夫去十多公里以外的讨赖河背水。盛夏时节，金黄的麦子无人收割，眼看要烂在地里。

这时候，有一位白胡子老人，声称有办法找到水。

老人说：只要监工答应他一个条件，他就能就地开泉出水！

老人的条件被答应了，修筑长城的一半民夫，回到了自己的家园收割打碾。

只见老人猫下腰，顺手抓起一把小石头，然后往空中一撒。无数的小石头象飞似的，在空中打了几个旋旋，咕噜噜跌落在关下的石滩上了。众民夫蜂拥而去看稀奇。只见一粒粒石子直往地下钻，发出“呼呼”的声响。一股股泉水哗哗往外淌。泉眼越来越大，水流得越来越多，民夫欣喜若狂。人们找老人时，老人早已无影无踪。由于关下泉眼很多，数也数不清，人们就叫“九眼泉”。

There is a nine-eye spring at the foot of Jiayu Pass, the water is clear & endless all the year round. The scenery is beautiful.

It's said when building Jiayu Pass, tens of thousands of labourers crowded together, dust flying and rolling, drinking water became the biggest problem. Without water, the project will be delayed! So the feudal official transferred many labourers to carry water on their back ten miles away. In mid Summer, the ripen wheat would soon get rotted as nobody reaped it.

Just then, a white-bearded old man claimed that he could find water.

The old man said: he would dredge spring and get water as long as the supervisor could accept one condition.

The condition was accepted, half of the labourers building the Great Wall came back home to reap their wheat.

They saw the old man bent down, grasped a handful of screes and then threw them into the air, the screes flew out and rotated in the air and fell on the stone beach. The laborers crowded there to watch the rarity: grains of scree digging into the earth with the sound of “Huu, Huu”, and streams of water gushing out. The spring eyes were becoming bigger and the water more and more. The workers were overjoyed. The old man had disappeared before they could find him. As there were so many spring eyes that people call it:“Nine-eye Spring”.

天下雄关碑

Stone Tablet of the Great Pass Under Heaven

在嘉峪关正门西100米处的大道南侧，竖立着一块大石碑，碑高三米，上刻的“天下雄关”四个大字，高度概括了嘉峪关的雄伟壮丽。

据说，在清朝嘉庆十四年，公元1809年，甘肃镇总兵李廷臣，在一个天高云淡的早晨，驱马扬鞭，来到嘉峪关视察防务。他观察这座屹立于戈壁沙漠之中的关城，越看越觉得气势真是雄伟，心情十分激动，便随口感赋：“真乃天下雄关！”，从关城回到游击衙门，他依然兴致勃勃，叫随从拿出纸墨，欣然命笔，写了“天下雄关”四个刚劲有力的大字。嘉峪关游击熊敏等人觉得这个题词形象地概述了嘉峪关的雄姿，便找人将这四个大字刻于碑上，并刻上署款小字，立于关城之西古驿道旁。《甘肃志·建置志》载：“嘉峪关东关坊西一里道左，嘉庆十四年有碑题曰：‘天下雄关’”。

At the south side of the road at 100 meters west of Jiayu Pass front Gate, there erects a huge 3-meter-high stone tablet with inscription of four characters: “Great Pass Under Heaven”.

It's said that in the 14th year of Jia Qing of the Qing Dynasty, the year 1809, Li Yanchen, general of Gansu Town, rode to Jiayu Pass for an inspection in a clear morning, seeing the Pass erecting in the dessert, he felt the majesty all the more and excitedly sang: “it is really a great Pass under Heaven”. Returned, he wrote four characters in high spirit: “Great Pass Under Heaven”. Xiong Min and others, guerillas of Jiayu Pass, thought the epigraph vividly summarized the grandeur of Jiayu Pass and had the characters and also the small signature engraved on the Tablet, then made it stand at the side of post road, west of Jiayu Pass.

宝　　碑 Precious Stone Tablet

嘉峪关城内保存着许多珍贵的石碑。其中有一块罕见的小石碑，高只有三十多公分，宽二十多公分。碑的上端和左右两边均刻写字迹。碑为墨绿色，表面非常光滑，象镜子一样铿亮，是用玉石刻制成的，人称“宝碑”。

相传，宝碑安放在北敌楼内的一个砖砌的台子上，四周栏杆护卫，面对着终年白雪皑皑的祁连山。每当雨后天晴，敌楼门一开，阳光射了进来，稍过片刻，对面祁连雪峰和山坡上的各种树木就从铮亮的石碑上映照出来，看得清清楚楚，活灵活现。

当年，远近的游人络绎不绝，不顾远途跋涉，来到嘉峪雄关，登上北敌楼，争相观看碑中胜景，无不感到惊奇。可惜，这块宝碑在解放前被人盗走了。

There saved lots of precious stone tablets inside the Jiayu Castle. One of them is a rare small stone tablet with the height of over 30 cm and width of over 20 cm. There are engraved characters on top and on both sides of it. The tablet is greenish black with smooth surface like a mirror, it's made of jade and people call it "Precious Tablet".

It's said the Precious Tablet was placed at a brick platform of the northern enemy tower, facing the snow-gleaming Qilian Mountain, guardrail protected around. When the day clears up and the gate is open, the sunshine penetrates into it, after a while, the trees in Qilan Mountain &slope are reflected from the shiny tablet, clear and vivid.

In those years, travelers far and near kept pouring in, regardless of the traipse, they came to Jiayu Pass and climbed up the tower to look at the scene in the tablet and nobody was not surprised. Unfortunately, the Tablet was stolen before Liberation.

嘉 峪 晴 烟 Jiayu Smoking Scenes in Clear Days

嘉峪晴烟是肃州八景之一。《重修肃州新志》载:“嘉峪晴烟,嘉峪在酒泉西,以其出玉,又谓玉石山,即汉遮虏障处。草树郁葱,云霄杳霭,每天宇晴霁,烟景苍翠,呈奇显秀,有可爱者。”

明代诗人戴弁的《嘉峪晴烟》曾写道:

烟笼嘉峪碧岧峣, 影拂昆仑万里遥。
暖气常浮春不老, 寒光欲散雪初消。
雨收远岫和云湿, 风度疏林带雾飘。
最是晚来闲望处, 夕阳天外锁山腰。

传说,当年修建嘉峪关的几万民夫,露天设灶,蓬蒿为柴,戈壁滩上烟雾弥漫。虽然工完人散,这些烟雾却风吹不散,雨打不断,越遇晴天越是显眼。

有一年,窜来一帮流寇。他们在距关十里的地方发现关内烟雾缭绕,流寇头目立即下令撤退。

有人问他:“未见一兵一卒,为何要撤?”

头目说:“难道你等未看见,晴空万里,哪来迷雾?显然有大军正在造饭。”大家一看,果然如此。

Jiayu smoking scenes in clear days is one of the scenes of Suzhou. It's recorded:“situation of Jiayu smoking scenes in clear days, is at west of Jiuquan. Grass and trees are verdant, brumes are distant and unclear in the sky. When it clears up, the greenery is green and lush in a smoking scene, showing its oddness and elegancy”.

Poet Dai Mou of the Ming Dynasty wrote in his poem Jiayu Smoking Scenes in Clear Days:

Jiayu under the smoke is bright and charming, the shadow of Kun Lun Mountain is far far away;

The Spring stays there long with warm airs, when the snow begins to melt, the cold days are going away.

The rain hides the distant mountains and wet clouds, the wind blows the sparse trees with flying fog.

The best scene is to look over in distance at an idle dusk, the setting Sun were as if locked at the waist of the mountain.

It's said that tens of thousands of labourers cooked in the open air and made the Gobi full of smoke which could not be terminated in rain or wind and was even more conspicuous in clear days.

李 陵 碑 Li Ling Tablet

在嘉峪关东北的长城外边，有一块方圆数十里的草湖滩，人们称为二分海子。海子里的土墩，人们叫它"李陵碑"。

传说汉武帝时，骑都尉李陵率领将士五千余人，在酒泉、张掖一带训练骑射，以备匈奴来犯。贰师将军李广要征伐大宛，武帝召李陵欲使为贰师将军押运辎重。李陵不愿意，遂上书武帝，请自率一队兵马，以少击众。

李陵打了胜仗，凯旋而归。路过二分海子的时候，李陵看见湖滩中水草茂密，四面沙丘回护，是个屯兵的好地方，便命令在此宿营。

李陵让将士运土填湖，构筑墩台。经过二十多天，在湖滩中心夯筑了一座黄土墩台。李陵亲笔书写了"誉满边关"四个大字，落款为"骑都尉李少卿题"，然后立碑于墩台之上。此碑于1989年倒塌。

李陵的骄奢淫逸，造成了后来的兵败被擒。

There is a grass lake shoal outside the Great Wall at the Northeast of Jiayu Pass, people called it Erfen Haizi. The mound in Haizi are called "Li Ling Tablet".

It's said at the time of Emperor Wu of the Han Dynasty, Li Ling was QiDuWei (an rank). He led over 5000 officers & soldiers to practise horse-riding and shooting in order to defend Xiongnu. General Li Guangli was to go on a punitive expedition to Dawan. Emperor Wu called in Li Ling to let him escort in transportation of weapon. Li Ling was not willing, so he wrote to Emperor Wu and asked to lead on a team to fight the numerous enemy.

Li Ling defeated the enemy and returned triumphantly. When passing by Erfen Haizi, Li Ling saw floating grass flourishing in the lake shoal which was protected by sand dunes around, an ideal place for stationing troops. He ordered to spend nights there. Then he was in a zeal to fill the lake with earth to build a mound platform. The officers& soldiers built a mound platform in the center of the lake shoal after over 20 days' toil & tire. Li Ling personally wrote "Wide Reputation at the Frontier", then inscribed "by QiDuWei Young Officer Li" and had the tablet erected on the platform. The tablet was lost.

His arrogance, extravagance, loose and leisure caused his failure and capture.

左 公 柳

Zuo Gong Willows

如今，当人们漫游于丝绸古道，从嘉峪关到新疆，处处都可以看到郁郁葱葱的杨柳，人们亲切地称为“左公柳”。

左公者，左宗堂是也，湖南湘阴人，对植树颇有偏爱。自古河西种树最为难事，左公进兵新疆讨伐阿古柏的分裂叛乱时，命令军队沿途遍栽杨柳，泾川以西，竟然形成道柳“连绵数千里绿如帷幄”的塞外奇观。左公不但植树，而且严加管理。左宗堂凯旋返回酒泉后，一农民骑驴进城办事，将毛驴栓在树上，毛驴悠闲自得地啃着树皮，无人过问。左宗堂下令在鼓楼前将毛驴斩首。通告：“若再有驴毁坏树木，驴同驴主同罪，格杀勿论。”左公斩驴护树传为佳话。

据载，清光绪四年(1878年)，杨昌浚等应邀来此酬办军务，看到一路绿树成荫，在一棵柳树刻过这样一首诗：

大将筹边未肯还，湖湘子弟满天山。

新栽杨柳三千里，引得春风度玉关。

嘉峪关文化旅游景区仍保留着几棵高大的“左公柳”。

Now, when people roaming along the Silk Road from Jiayu Pass to Xin Jiang, they will see verdant willows everywhere, and people kindly call them “Zuo Gong Willows”. Zuo Gong fought for the insurrection of A Gubai, he ordered his army to plant willows along the road and actually formed the frontier miracle. Besides, he was strict at management. A farmer rode a donkey downtown for business, he tied the donkey to a tree, the donkey gnawed the bark of the tree at will. Seeing this, Zuo Gong ordered to behead the donkey. This “beheading donkey for protecting the tree” has become a much-told story.

It’s recorded that in 1878 Yang Changjun etc were invited to make preparations for military affairs, seeing the shady greenery along, he carved a poem on the bark of a willow:

The general did not return after the war and there are his soldiers everywhere in Tian Shan Mountain. The newly planted willows of thousands of miles attract the Spring breeze to the Frontier.

In Jiayu Pass Culture & Tourism Scenery Zone still remain a few lofty “Zuo Gong Willows”.

嘉峪关之所以被称之为长城沿线保存最完整，规模最宏大的军事防御体系，与当时严密科学的施工管理，有着直接的关系。

1975年，在嘉峪关北的一段长城内发现了一块工牌，它告诉我们，当时修筑长城的时候，采取了责任到人的办法，把刻写有施工队领队姓名和起止年月日的工牌，埋于所筑城墙之内，如果城墙倒塌、破损，就按工牌所记的工段和施工队，来追查责任。

由于采取了承包责任制，长城的修筑加快了工期。据历史资料记载：从卯来泉到野麻湾50多公里的长城，只用了一年多的时间就完成了。

“边墙上头多冻雀，侵晓霜明星渐落”。一望无际的大轱辘车在戈壁荒原上行进，黄土弥漫了整个天空，尘埃落尽，一座雄伟壮丽的嘉峪关，横空出世。

The reason why Jiayu Pass is called the most complete and the largest-scale military defense system remained along the great Wall is directly connected with the strictly scientific construction and management at the time.

In 1975,a working Tabula was found under the Great Wall north of Jiayu Pass. It tells us that they adopted the system of division of responsibility when building the Great Wall. They buried the Tabula inside the wall they built. If the wall collapsed or was damaged, the responsibility will be found out according to the section and construction team recorded on the Tabula. The construction of the Great Wall speeded up because of the system of division of responsibility.

“There are many frozen sparrows on the Wall, the fog is heavy when the stars become disappearing”. The dust will penetrate in the air when the big Wheel Cart marches on in the stretch-to-the -horizon Gobi and you will see a majestic Jiayu Pass as the dust falls to the ground.

工　牌

Working Tabula

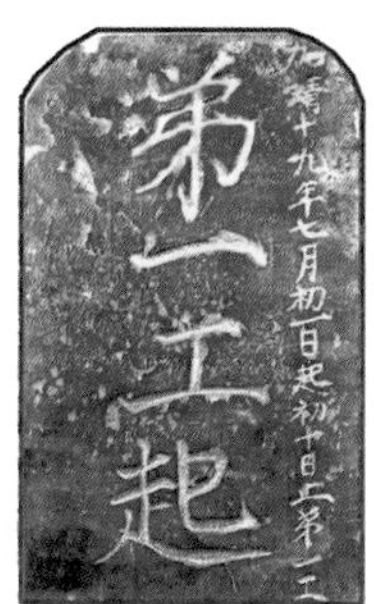

正面

反面

城　壕

The Moat

关城外有一道壕，又叫护城河。现存壕长300余米，上阔10.6米，下宽2.2米，距外城墙不足1米。壕外还修有一道1米高的土堰。据《肃州志》记载，还有外壕、远墙各一道，现已无存。关外10余米处有一小阜，皆沙砾堆成，状如月城。阜长157.8米，宽35米，高3-6米，可掩护关城。在月城附近，早年设置梅花六角坑，俗称“绊马坑”。古时阵地作战，常以生铁铸成多角形，状似蒺藜子，埋在坑内，成为陷阱。在修建关城的时候，还建筑了通讯指挥墩、旗墩和闸门墩。

Outside the Pass, there is a moat with the remained length of 300 meters, a width of 10.6 meters above and 2.2meters below. It is less than a meter away from the outer wall. An earthen dam of a meter high was built outside the moat. More than ten meters outside the Pass, there is a mound piled with sand and pebbles, shaping like a moon. The mound is 157.8 meters long, 35 meters wide and 3~6meters high. It could protect the Pass. Near the mound, there were six-corner pits like plum-blossoms, which are called "Tripping-horse Pits" popularly.

祁 连 峡 谷

Qilian Canyon

北大河又名讨赖河，古称“呼蚕水”。该河发源于青海祁连山讨赖掌峡谷，河水从珠龙关出峡后，流经嘉峪关。

嘉峪关境内的讨赖河，深达80米以上的大峡谷，险峻天成，气势宏伟。谷内流水喧嚣，岸边长城蜿蜒，雪山耸峙。万里长城第一墩立于悬崖之上，登高远望，嘉峪雄关尽收眼底，大漠风光苍苍茫茫，河山揽胜，美不胜收。

Bei Da River is also called Tao Lai River, and “Hu Can Water” in history. It originates from Tao Lai Zhang canyon of the Qilian Mountain in Qinghai; the water flows past Jiayu Pass. The over-80-meter-deep big canyon of Tao Lai River inside Jiayu Pass is naturally steep and imposing with noisy flows inside the canyon, wandering Great Wall and snow mountains at its banks, the First Beacon Platform of the Great Wall standing on the cliff. Ascending a height to look the distant view, you will have a panoramic view of the Great Pass and the vast dessert. The breath-taking prospects of the land are really a feast to eyes.

南 山 积 雪

Snows on the Southern Mountain

嘉峪关正南的祁连山，四季有雪，千古不消，凝华积素，争奇献秀，凌空万仞，望之如堆琼垒玉。尤其在嘉峪关下观赏祁连雪峰，青砖与白雪，楼宇与冰峰，构成了一幅绝美的图画。

In the Qilian Mountains south of Jiayu Pass, it snows all the year round and never melts; the snow is extremely high up in the air just like piling jade. Especially seen at the foot of Jiayu Pass, the black bricks & white snow, the buildings & ice pinnacles form a superb picture.

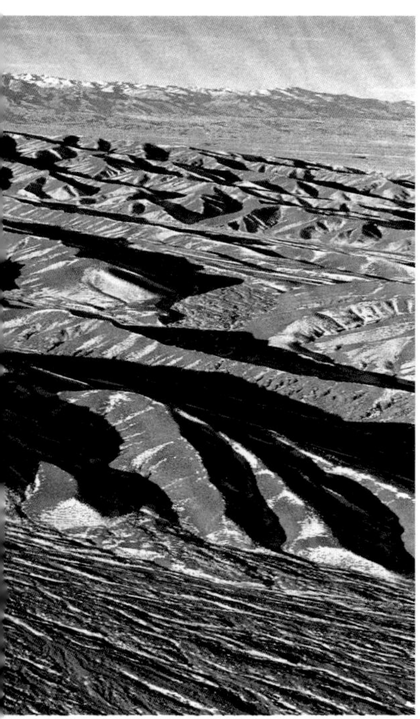

关 限 华 夷

Pass Restricting the Western Foreigners

《重修肃州新志》中说:“关限华夷即嘉峪关也。先年只有关城,无楼。河南武陟李端澄构大楼,以壮伟观,望之四达,犹未有长城也。后因大学士翟銮巡边,兵备付使李涵又议筑长城以限西夷。于是,关之南北限以长城,长城之中,边寨有楼,以镇西夷。登之,猛然感慕汉光武闭玉门关,以谢西域之事。徘徊瞻眺,真天限华夷者也。诸公卿题咏亦多”。此为肃州后八景之一,高度概括了嘉峪关的雄伟壮丽和夺人魂魄的气势。

Revised Suzhou Record says: Restricting the Western Foreigners refers to Jiayu Pass. There were no buildings except the castle in the early years. After a big building was built by Li Duancheng, the view was unblocked and there was not the Great Wall. Later the Great Wall was built to restrict the Western foreigners. So the North and South of the Pass was divided by the Great Wall. Inside there were towers in the frontier villages to pacify the west foreigners. Many poets and bookmen intoned poems about it. It late became one of the eight scenes of Suzhou as it highly outlines the majesty & splendor and the appalling momentum of Jiayu Pass.

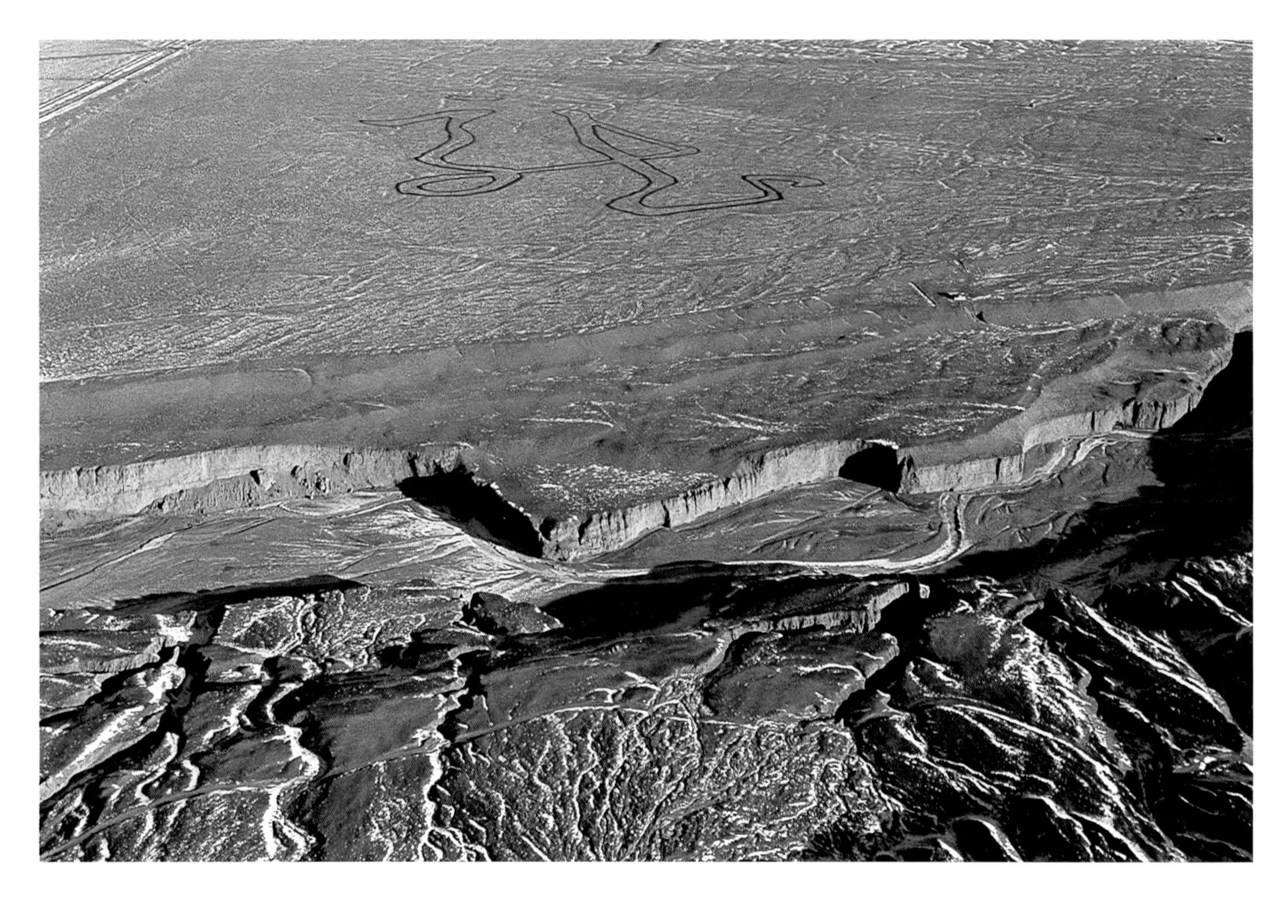

世 纪 龙 林 Century Dragon Forest

在嘉峪关长城第一墩东侧广阔的戈壁滩上，由嘉峪关市人民政府、凤凰卫视、北大资源集团共同策划和实施的“世纪龙林”工程，是在世纪龙年，采用唐代书法家怀素的草书“龙”，在长城下开挖长1000米、宽800米、笔画宽2米的“龙”字，以“雄关烽火绘巨龙”的大型活动闻名于世。1999年12月31日，“龙”字开挖成形，2000年填土植树。目前，世纪龙林已全面完成了植树造林任务，成为嘉峪关下的又一旅游景点。据悉，这个“龙”字是世界上书写于大地之上的最大的汉字。

On the broad Gobi, east side of the First Platform of the Great Wall at Jiayu Pass, the project of “Century Dragon Forest”, jointly planned and implemented by the Phoenix TV, Resources Group of Beijing University and the People’s Government of Jiayuguan City, was digging out the huge character “龙” with its length of 1000 meters, width of 800 meters and strokes width of 2 meters under the Great Wall in the Dragon year of the century, by adopting the grass style character “龙” by Huai Su, the calligrapher of Tang Dynasty. On Dec. 31 of 1999, the Character “龙” was dug into sight. In 2000, we filled the character with earth and planted trees above. Now the tree-planting at the Century Dragon Forest has been finished and it has become another scenic spot of the Pass. It’s known that the character “龙” is the largest made out on the earth.

石 峡 天 险

The Steep Gorge

位于嘉峪关市区15公里处的黑山，有一天然峡谷，陡峭险峻，峡谷最窄处，只有10多米。谷内流水潺潺，牧草茂密，闻名遐迩的丝绸之路曾从这里经过，自古以来，这里就是使节商胡东西往来的通道。明嘉靖十八年（公元1539年），利用黑山天险，在峡口修筑南北两截长城，封锁山口。其北面的石壁上楷书双阴线刻“北漠尘清”四字，左旁刻“大明万历癸巳肃州兵备广陵郭师古书”。

There is a natural steep gorge in the Black Mountain 25 km away from downtown Jiayuguan city, with the narrowest width of only over 10 meters. There are murmuring flows and flourishing grass inside the gorge and the famous Silk Road passed through here. From old times, this has been a passage for the envoys & merchants to come back and forth. In 1539, two sections of north & south Great Wall were built at the gorge mouth to block the mountain pass by aid of the steepness of the Black Mountain. There are carved characters on the north Wall.

悬 壁 长 城

The Great Wall Overhanging

在嘉峪关城楼西北约6公里处有一段长城，依山势而建，直至黑山山顶，远远看去，墙体如悬挂山间，故称“悬壁长城”。又因这段长城的形势与八达岭十分相似，被称为“西部八达岭”。它是嘉峪关军事防御体系的一部分，与峡口南的“暗壁”长城配合，封锁石关峡，它上面的烽火台与峡口南的两座烽火台照应联络，传递军情。悬壁长城就地取材，用山上的石片和山下的黄土分层砌筑，坚固美观。

At 6 kilometers northwest of Jiayu Pass gate tower, a section of the Wall was built along the landform of the mountain till to the top of the black Mountain and it looks like a wall suspending in the mountain, thus it's called "The Great Wall Overhanging" and also called "Ba Da Ling in the West" as its landform is very identical to that of Ba Da Ling. It works together with the "hidden wall" of south gorge mouth to block Shi Guan Gorge. The material of the Great Wall in Suspension came from the local mountain stone pieces and loess, solid and artistic.

长城第一墩

The First Beacon Platform of the Great Wall

嘉峪关长城第一墩，又称讨赖河墩，肃州兵备道李涵于明嘉靖十八年(1539年)监筑，因墩台耸立于西长城尽头、讨赖河北岸高达82米的悬崖峭壁之上，故名之。长城第一墩担负着传递嘉峪关南至祁连山方面的敌情信息的任务。该墩台筑于长城内侧二米处，残迹高约7米，底部呈不规则正方形。南北宽和东西长均为14.5米。墩体为黄土夹沙夯筑，夯层15厘米。

站在长城第一墩上，风光无限。长城美景、讨赖河大峡谷、壮丽的祁连山尽收眼底。同时，嘉峪关险要的地理位置也一目了然。

The First Beacon Platform of the Great Wall is called TaoLai He Platform, built under the supervision of Li Han in 1539. It's named as it stands at the end of the West Wall, on top of the 82-meter cliff north of Tao Lai River. It worked as a messenger to pass information of enemy situation from south Jiayu Pass to Qilian Mountains. The platform is situated at 2 meters inner side of the Wall. The remnant is 7 meters high with irregular square bottom, its width and length are both 14.5 meters. Standing on the First Platform of the Great Wall, you will have a panoramic picture of the Wall, the grand gorge of Tao Lai River and the majestic Qilian Mountains.

内　　城 The Inner City

嘉峪关内城是嘉峪关的心脏，居于关城正中。内城的基础就是明洪武五年冯胜将军下河西选址修筑的土城。经明正德元年和嘉靖十八年两次增筑，形成了现在保存下来的形胜。在明代，内城设有军政指挥机关，开始称守备司，后来叫游击将军府。还有检验出入关证件的机关，名为嘉峪关公馆。关内原有夷厂、仓库等建筑，存放军火武器、草料、粮秣。内城在整个关城中处于要害部位，“辎重及重心皆在正方形中”。内城的平面为西头大、东头小的梯形，象一个大斗。西城墙长166米，东城墙长154米，南北城墙各长约160米，周长640米。

内城墙的城台、敌台和垛口等处用砖包砌，其余部分都是黄土夯筑。

The Inner City of Jiayu Pass is the heart of Jiayu Pass. It's located at the center of the castle. It's foundation was the earth city built by General Feng Sheng. The Inner City became what it is now after two time's expansions. There were many buildings like Guerilla General Mansion, Jiayu Pass Mansion, factories and warehouses. It was the key situation in the whole castle. Its plane is a trapezia with a bigger west and a smaller east like a big dipper. The west wall is 166 meters long, the east 154m, south and north are both 160m, the perimeter is 640m.

The Platform, enemy platform and stack mouth were laid with bricks and the rest were built with earth.

游击将军府 Guerrilla General Mansion

游击将军府初建于明隆庆年间(十六世纪中期)。游击将军府坐北向南,总面积约有3,000平方米。据有关资料记载,府门朝南开,为红漆大门。门前有一座五彩牌坊。门东西两边筑有两个高台。台上有两座小房和一间式门房。台上两边建有高大的彩画钟楼和鼓楼。府前马路以南原来筑有大照壁一座,坐南向北,高约4米,宽约6米。照壁用土坯砌筑成。壁面白灰做底,尽墙画有一条大虎,着深驼色。此照壁使游击将军府显得更威严。进红漆大门,是两套院子,前厅除过厅外,东西各五间,为衙门府。后厅是办公处和住室,有红漆明柱前廊。院内正厅五间,陪房八间,过厅五间,呈四合院,占地面积1,008平方米。今游击将军府为现代重修。

The Guerrilla General Mansion was built in the year of the Long Qing of Ming Dynasty, facing the south with a total construction area of about 3000 square meters. It's recorded that its door opened southward and was painted in red and there was a 5-color memorial archway in front of the door, there were two high platforms in east and west side of the door. Two small rooms and one gate house were on the platform, and a tall Bell Tower and Drum Tower were built at both sides of the platform. Entering the red door, there were two courtyards, in the front Hall there were 5 rooms in each side of the east and west used as yamen mansion except the passing hall. The back Hall was used as offices and living place and now only the back Hall is still kept here. There are 5 main halls, 5 minor rooms and 5 passing halls, in a form of quadrangle with total area of 1008 square meters. The present Guerrilla General Mansion was rebuilt in modern times.

罗　　城 Luo City

罗城砖包城墙长191.3米，底基厚25米，上阔5.3米，高10.5米。基础用坚硬的麻子石石条砌筑，极为坚固。墙的正中设有关的正门，这是古代进关的第一道城门。上面嵌有乾隆皇帝题的“嘉峪关”三字。门洞为砖砌拱券式，基础和通道用石条砌铺。门洞深25米，高6米，宽4米，有黑漆铁皮包钉双扇门。罗城内侧南端有一条宽阔的砖铺马道，直通城顶。登上城头，可以看到迎敌一面的防御性建筑。在190余米长的城头筑垛口一百三十三个，全用砖砌筑。每个垛墙高1.5米，宽1.7米，阔60厘米。垛的中间设一正方形瞭望孔，还设有灯槽。灯槽共有一百二十二个。每个灯槽下有一个斜坡式的射击孔。

The Wall of Luo City is 191.3 m long, its base is 25 m thick, the upper 5.3broad,and 10.5 m high. The base is built with firm stone plates which is extremely solid. There was a front gate in the center of the Wall and this is the first gate for entering the Pass. There was inserted characters“嘉峪关” inscribed by Emperor Qianlong. The gate hole is 25 m deep, 6 m high and 4 m wide, the two doors are wrapped by black painted iron sheets. There was a broad horse way paved with bricks in the south and at the inner side of Luo city, leading to the top. Ascending the top of the city wall, you will see defense construction. There were 133 battlements on the over 190-meter-long city wall, all made of bricks. Each battlement wall is 1.5 m high, 1.7 m wide and 60 cm broad. There was a square watch hole in the center of every battlement, as well as light groove. There were 122 light grooves, under each was a sloping shooting hole.

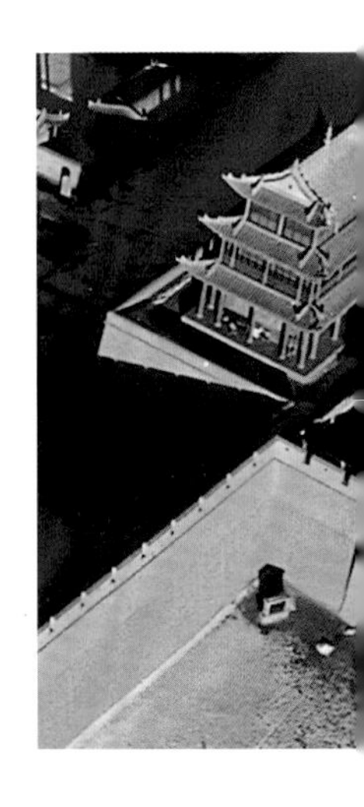

瓮　　城 Court City

内城东西门外均有瓮城护卫，门向南开，不与内城门直通，增添了关城幽深肃穆的气势。瓮城墙用黄土夯筑，与内城墙同高，并与内城墙迂回衔接，浑为一体。城门洞为砖砌拱券式，门洞基础和过道用石条砌铺。城门用黑漆铁皮包钉。东西瓮城门上建阁楼各一座。阁楼高5.7米，坐北向南，面积28.6平方米。阁楼为一层小三间式，楼前有红漆明柱通廊，两边与城墙相通。对扇小门向南开，东西两边开窗。楼脊扣筒瓦。楼顶四角檐上装龙首瓦，檐翼起翘，美观大方。西瓮城与罗城墙中间，原有木制渡槽状“天桥”一座，把内城、瓮城和罗城衔接起来，便于战时集结兵力，运送弹药。现在虽然“天桥”无存，但遗迹尚在。

外　　城 The Outer City

关城之东、南、北三面有黄土夯筑的围墙，称外城。其西端与罗城相接，南北连接肃州西长城，与长城成犄角之势，互相呼应，便于防守。东部围墙沿岩岗边缘筑起，内部有一广场，使整个关城形成龟状，构成六面掩护之势，建筑十分得法。外城墙长1，100米，残高3.8米，底宽1.5米，上阔0.65米。南北墙与内城墙相平行，中间有一车马道。东墙残缺383米，现已补筑。并增筑了垛墙和瞭望孔，恢复了原貌。垛墙每垛宽1米，高0.75米，厚0.35米。瞭望孔宽0.12米，高0.20米，厚0.35米。外城墙是嘉靖十八年(1539年)构筑关城南北之长城时增筑的。

The bounding-wall in east, south and north of the Pass are called the Outer City. Its west end connects Luo city, its north & south neighbor the west Wall of Suzhou, forming a horn to echo each other, convenient for defense. The east bounding-wall was built from the edge of rock and the square inside it makes the whole Pass in a form of a turtle for protection in 6 directions. The construction was very reasonable. The Outer City Wall is 1,000 m long, its relic is 3.8 m high, bottom 1.5 m wide and the upper is 0.65 m broad. The north-south wall is parallel to that of Inner City Wall and there was a carriage way between them. There were 383 m in deformity in the east Wall and now it has been repaired and the battlement and watch holes have been added and restored to its old look. The battlement is 1 m wide, 0.75 m high and 0.35 m thick; the watch hole is 0.12m wide, 0.20 m high and 0.35 thick. The Outer City wall was added in 1539 when building the north-south Wall.

There was the Court City for protection outside the west &east gate of the Inner City. Its door opened southward. It was not directly connected to the Inner City. This added the atmosphere of serenity and solemnity of the City. The wall of the court city was built with earth and was as high as that of the Inner City, and connected to it by roundabout way and then became an integral whole. There was an attic on each of the eastern gate and the western gate, 5.7 m high, facing the south and with total area of 28.6 square meters. The attic was a 3-room floor with visible columns in front and was connected with the Wall at both sides. The dragon-head tiles were installed at the 4 eaves with their wing raising, pleasant to eyes and in good taste.

城　　门 City Gates

嘉峪关内城有东西二门，二门遥相对峙，甚有气派。面对茫茫戈壁的正门之上书写“嘉峪关”三个字，更是气势磅礴。嘉峪关城门的门洞基础和过道均用长方形石条砌筑。门洞长20.8米，宽4.2米。门洞为砖砌拱券式，皆为四平四立，据说这是国门的规格。明时，国力衰退，筑嘉峪关为西疆。有民谣说：出了嘉峪关，两眼泪不干。由此可以想见，出了嘉峪关，就已经是背井离乡。同时也说明了嘉峪关在明代军事地位的重要。

城门为木制，黑漆铁皮包钉，坚固而森严。

The inner city has an eastern gate and a western gate, which are opposite with each other from far away.

There are three Chinese characters“嘉峪关”of great momentum written above the main gate which faces the boundless Gobi. The gate base and the passway were built with oblong stone-plates. With the length of 20.8 meters and the width of 4.2 meters, the gate holes are arc-shaped with bricks laid four lying after four standing, which is said to be the standard of the nation gate.

The gate doors were made of wood, covered with big nails and black-painted iron sheets. They are solid and severe.

三　　楼 The Three Towers

内城有东西二门。东门之上的楼宇称“光华楼”，有紫气东升，光华普照的意思。西门之上的楼宇称“柔远楼”，是安定边陲的意思。正门之上的楼宇称“嘉峪关楼”。“光华”、“柔远”两楼均修筑于公元1507年。“嘉峪关楼”修筑于公元1495年。三楼筑于9米高的城台之上，高均为17米。楼为三层三檐式建筑，面宽三间，进深两间，周围是红漆明柱的回廊。最底层是砖木结构，基砌石条。东西两面开门，有石条铺砌台阶。楼内安装木楼梯，沿梯可登二、三层楼。二、三楼均为木结构，周围木格壁窗。楼顶为歇山式，脊上装蟠龙、狮子等兽形瓦。整个楼阁雕梁画栋，五彩缤纷，有诗云：“磨砖砌就鱼鳞瓦，五彩装成碧玉楼。”

The building above the eastern gate of the inner city is called “Gonghua Tower”, the building above the western gate is called “Rouyuan Tower”, the building above the main entrance is called “Jiayuguan Tower”. The former two buildings were built in 1507. The last one was built in 1495. With the same height of 17 meters, the three buildings sit on a platform of a meter high. with three storeys and three eaves, each building has three rooms in the front, two rooms in the back. With carved beams and painted rafters, the whole building litters colourfully.

官　　井 The Official Well

关城中偏西北有官井一眼，上装有辘轳一架，并建有井亭。虽已无法考证开凿年代，但据说是明代建关时打的井，供城内守备官兵使用的。在解放前的几十年时间里，关内无人居住；本世纪五十年代后期，城楼下打了数眼机井，由于水位下降，关内的井就干涸了。关城内西北角上，距官井30米处，原来还有一眼民用井，现遗迹无存。

There is an official well by the northwest in the castle. Above it is a windlass and a pavilion. It is said that the well was dig when building the Pass.

The pavilion existed in the former years. During the last years of 50's of this century, a few wells were dug at the foot of the castle. Because of the lowing down of the water level, the official well became dry. The pavilion was blown down by the wind.

戏　　台 The Play Platform

戏台位于东瓮城门外，坐南面北。戏台为清乾隆五十七年（公元1792年）修筑。戏台面宽三间，进深两间，面积114平方米。屏风上有一楹联，上书"时雨助王师直教万里昆仑争迎马迹；春风怀帝力且嘉十年帷幄重扶刀环"。上下联题有小字，分别为"光绪十年仲冬"，"邵阳魏炳蔚敬佩"。戏台两侧还有砖砌屏风，上刻对联："离合悲欢演往事；愚贤忠佞认当场"。

The play platform is situated outside the gate of the eastern court city. It was built in the 57th year of Qianlong in the Qing Dynasty. With an area of 114 square meters, the building has two front rooms and two back rooms. Above the play platform, the top was made with wooden criss-crosses, with the Eight Diagrams Pictures being painted on. The front and the back platforms were divided by a wooden screen on which eight immortals' pictures were painted and a couplet was written at the two sides of the platform. Colourful frescos were painted on the walls.

关 帝 庙 The God Guan Temple

关帝庙是嘉峪关庙宇之中规模最大的建筑。据记载，关帝庙是明正德元年(1506年)修建嘉峪关内城东西二楼时修建的。从明末到清代，关帝庙曾多次扩建，庙内有大殿一座，陪殿二座，穿庭一座，牌楼一座，总建筑面积约720平方米。陪殿内各墙壁上，画满了三国故事彩画。关帝庙的建筑幸存下来的只有牌楼一座。据《嘉峪关调查记》："入内，右侧有关帝庙，匾额累累，额上文字如'长城主宰'等。出庙门，旁有'重修关帝庙'碑文"。"长城主宰"的匾额现存嘉峪关内。

The God Guan Temple is the largest of the Jiayuguan temple buildings. It was built in the first year of Zheng de in the Ming Dynasty (1506). After being rebuilt for many times, the temple now has a main hall, two secondary halls, a passing court, and an archway, with the area of 720 square meters. There were earthen God statues etc. in the temple. Only the archway of the God Guan Temple survives.

文 昌 阁 Wenchang Attic

文昌阁距东瓮城门14.9米，为明代建筑，清道光二年(1822)年重建。在二楼中间檩上写有："大清道光二年岁次壬午秋八月，署嘉峪关营游击金城张怀辅、分驻嘉峪关巡检西蜀张恒利重建"。二楼西侧檩上还有"帝道遐昌"、"皇图巩固"两条题字。文昌阁楼为石条砌基，基长11.9米，宽11米，面积130.4平方米。文昌阁为两层两檐歇山顶式。阁顶用筒瓦铺盖，阁檐四角均装有三个龙首、一条蟠龙。阁脊上下两端安装有蟠龙，三条脊共有蟠龙六条。文昌阁为二层小楼，每层两檐起翘。顶脊中间有个佛龛。阁的底层两侧各有砖砌小房一间，有老式对开门，门扇一绘画有门神。两房中间有一宽阔的门洞。阁外北侧有一木梯，供人们上下行走用。阁上书"文昌殿"，并悬"斯文主宰"匾额。阁下原有一匾，上写"出关大道"四字，今已不存。

14.9 meters away from the eastern gate of the court city, there is Wenchang attic built in the Ming Dynasty and rebuilt in the 2nd year of Daoguang (1822) of the Qing Dynasty. The attic is of the slow mountain type with two floors and two eaves. The top was covered with the semi-circle-shaped tiles. Three dragon heads and a curled-up dragon were set at the four corners of the eaves. On each of the three backs of the attic there are two curled-up dragons set at the two ends. There is a Buddha niche in the middle of the top back. A Door God was painted on a door of one of the two small houses built on the two sides of the attic.

At the northern side out of the attic, there is a wooden ladder for up and down. The Chinese Characters "文昌殿" were written on the attic.

东 闸 门

The Eastern Dam Gate

外城门矗立在外城东北的高岗边沿，又叫东闸门。门洞高4.2米，宽3.8米，深10.6米，两侧石条砌筑基础，砖砌壁，壁嵌三十六根方木支柱。门上建闸楼，面宽三间，进深两间，为单檐歇山顶式。

The outer city gate stands highly on the hillside northeast of the outer city. It is also called the Eastern Dam Gate. With a height of 4.2meters, width of 3.8meters and depth of 10. 6 meters, the gate has a stone-plate base in the two sides, a brick wall and 26wooden supporting pillars. Above the gate is a gate tower with 3 front rooms, two back rooms, a single eave and a slow mountain like top.

壕　　堑 The Exterior Moat

长城，是华夏文明在东方大地上刻写的不朽的形象。它存在的恒久，功能的显赫，影响的深远，是世界上任何文化遗迹无可比拟的。而它的组成部分壕堑，虽寂寞无名，但却是另一条看不见的战线。

在嘉峪关，壕堑作为重要的军事防御设施，经过近500年的风雨洗礼，几乎填满了沙尘，它的旧迹，无论在戈壁上，还是在高山险要之地，无处不在，走近它，历史的风霜扑面而来。

嘉峪关的外壕，长约15公里，从关南的讨赖河北岸起，蜿蜒向北，穿过平坦的戈壁一直延伸至黑山附近。遗迹上宽9.8米，下宽3.5米，深2.1米，据考证，当年壕沟的深度最少也有4米。

粗略地估计，这样的一条沟壕，挖取的土石量就有40多万立方米。无数的守边戍卒，无数的平民百姓，用简单的铁器，一块块、一段段地往下开凿，多少汗水，多少血泪，为历史，为长城，留下不可磨灭的见证。

The Great Wall is the immortal image of China's civilization carved on the Oriental Land. The eternity of its existence, brilliance of function, profound and lasting influence are unmatched to any of the culture heritages in the world. Its composing part, the moat, though unknown, is another invisible line.

In Jiayu Pass, Moat, as the important military defense facility, is almost filled with dust and sand through nearly 500 years of time and tide. Approaching its ruins wherever at the Gobi or at strategic mountain place, you will feel clearly the hardship of its history.

The exterior moat of Jiayu Pass is about 15 kilometers long. From the north bank of Tao Lai River, it wanders its way northward through the flat Gobi to nearby the Black Mountain. The relic is 9.8 meters wide on the top and 3.5 meters at the bottom, 2.1 meters deep. The textual research says the depth of the Moat in those years was at least 4 m. The cursory estimate says the earth measure for such a moat is over 400 thousand cubic meters. The countless soldiers and common people dug downward bit by bit with simple ironware. The sweats, bloods and tears have left indelible witness for history, for the Great Wall.

角 楼 The Corner Towers

城的四隅有角台，台上建有戍楼，是当时守城士兵放哨的地方。戍楼面积29.7平方米，高5.4米，二层单间式，全用砖砌成。楼顶无脊，建有平台。平台四周设垛，形如碉堡。戍楼一面有砖砌拱券小门，另三面开窗。楼内有木梯，可登上平台。

At the four corners of the city, there are corner platforms, on which are guard towers. They are places for soliders to stand sentry. All the buildings were built with bricks, and each one has an area of 29.7 square meters, height of 5.4meters, two storeys with one room on each. The top has no backs but a platform. Around the platform are battlements, looking like a blockhouse. On one side of the guard tower, there is an arc-shaped gate built with bricks. On the other three sides, windows were opened. There is a wooden ladder inside for up and down the platform.

箭 楼 The Arrow Tower

箭楼为嘉峪关之上的警戒哨所。箭楼高5.6米，西面有豁口，其他三面筑矮墙。楼上盖灰瓦，楼脊装蟠龙首瓦，飞檐凌空。关城之上碉堡林立，城楼高峙，显示出万里长城天下雄关的凛然姿态。

The arrow tower is a sentry place for alert. The height is 5.6 meters. It has a breach in the western side .The other three sides are short walls. The top was covered with grey tiles, the back set with tiles of curled-up dragons. The eaves fly highly in the air. On the Pass, the blockhouses one after one, the buildings high, it exhibits the awe-inspiring posture of the Greatest Pass under Heaven of the Great Wall.

马　　道 Horse Way

关城马道为青砖斜坡式，可从内城直上城顶。马道斜长22.2米，宽2.7米，马道下原有成排的拴马桩，现遗迹无存。

The horse way of the Pass was paved with dark greeh bricks as a slope, from which inside the inner city one could mount the city top. The slope is 22.2m long, 2.7m wide.At the foot of the way, there were poles for tieing horses, now no remnant exists.

敌　　楼 The Enemy Tower

嘉峪关南北城墙无门，墙头中段筑有南北二敌台，台上修有敌楼。两楼南北相望。敌楼面积38.2平方米，为一层三间带前廊式。

楼外明柱通廊与左右城墙相通。南北二敌楼是放置兵器的地方。本世纪四十年代，在北敌楼内置一墨绿玉石碑。

There are no gates in the southern and northern walls of the Jiayu Pass. On each middle part of the two walls, is an enemy platform, on it is an enemy tower. The two towers face with each other from south to north. With an area of 38.2 square meters, the tower has just one floor with three rooms and a front corridor.

The two towers were used to store weapons. In the 40's of this century, a green jade tablet was set in the northern tower.

马 道 门 楼 Horse way Tower

从内城进入马道，有砖石结构的门楼，门楼建筑精巧，青瓦铺顶，并有精美的瓦饰，气势森严。门楼内侧有照壁，绘有传统壁画。

Entering onto the horse way from the inner city, one could find a gate tower made of bricks and stone. The tower was ingeniously built with the top covered with dark green tiles and tile sculptures. The posture is severe. There is a Photo wall on the inner side of the tower, with traditional frescos painted on it.

林则徐出关 Lin Zexu Going out of the Pass

清道光二十二年九月初七，即公元1842年10月11日，林则徐因禁烟被“革去卿衔，道戍伊犁”路经嘉峪关。嘉峪关下，秋风瑟瑟，一派凄凉。“严关百尺界天西，万里征人驻马蹄。飞阁遥连秦树直，缭垣斜压陇云低。天山巉削摩肩立，瀚海苍茫入望迷，谁道崤函千古险，回头只见一丸泥。”，在目睹嘉峪关的一瞬，林则徐阴郁的心情豁然开朗，写下了脍炙人口、流传千古的《出嘉峪关感赋》四首。高度褒扬了嘉峪关的雄伟气势，表现了一个民族英雄的宽广胸怀。在嘉峪关短时间的逗留中，林则徐充满了无限的依恋，他在《塞外杂咏》中写道：

雄关楼堞依云开，驻马边墙首重回。
风雨满城人出塞，黄花真笑逐臣来。

On the 7th day September in the twenty-second year of Daoguang in the Qing Dynasty, Lin Zexu went by the Jiayu Pass to Yili because of being demoted for his ban-on-opium movement. His attachment to the Pass was expressed in one of his poems:

Pass and Towers spread with the clouds
Beside the wall stop my horse, turn my head back
Go out of the Pass when the rain falls
Yellow flowers smile when I come

双 井 子 Paring Wells

双井子堡，地处嘉峪关西20多公里，是嘉峪关西的前哨阵地，是关外第一防线的宿卫营盘。城堡周长708.3米，现存城墙586米，残高4.2米，底宽2.8米，上宽1.6米。城开二门，一门向东，一门向西，东门已残缺，西门楼台基遗迹清晰可见。门洞深10.5米，宽4米。楼台内侧有一斜坡马道，可登上城头。东墙外10米处有一庙宇遗址，现仅存庙台。

传说堡内原有水井数十眼，每两眼井紧挨一起，为一对。一对井中，一眼有水，一眼无水，称之为“真井”、“假井”。官兵驻守时，用真井，水源旺盛，人畜共饮。城堡陷落时，掩埋真井，露假井，断水源，使敌不能立足。

The Paring-well fort is situated more than 20 kilometers west from Jiayuguan city. The fort has a perimeter of 708.3 meters with the remnant wall of 586 meters long, 4.2 meters high, 2.8 meters wide below and 1.6 meters wide above. It has two gates, one facing east, the other west.

It is said that there were tens of wells in the fort. Two of them were next, as a pair. For a pair, one had water, the other hadn't, which were called “real well” and “false well”.When the soldiers were there, they used the real one. When the fort fell into enemy's hands, the real well had been buried, the false well appeared, and so the enemy had no water to use.

骟马城 Shanma City

位于甘肃玉门市玉门镇东南78公里的白土梁村。城宽60米，长65米，城墙底宽9米，顶宽5.2米，厚0.13～0.18米，高约10米，城堡矗立在马河西岸。在城南的一块高约10～15米的台地上，发现有一处古文化遗址，有灰层、墓葬及陶器等遗迹、遗物。在这里出土的陶器都是夹沙、褐色、手制的平底器，器形小件的较多。部分有火烧烟熏的痕迹，当为炊具。城内也发现有大量的红、灰陶片、绳纹砖及汉代黑砖、石磨等。现为省级文物保护单位。

骟马城由内城、外城、城壕等组成，东依马河深达数十丈的峡谷天险，进可攻、退可守。据专家考证，骟马城的修筑年代为汉代，唐、宋、清诸朝代均重修扩建。

Shanma City is located in Baituliang Village 78km southeast of Yumen Town .On an about 10-meter-high terrace in the south of the city, ancient ruins were found with relics such as grieshochs, tombs and pottery etc. Most of the Pottery unearthed here are flat-bottom utensils that are sand including, brown and handmade. Most of them are small ones. Some of them have traces of smoking and should be kitchenware. Great amount of red, grey pottery pieces, rope-line bricks and black bricks as well as stone mills of the Han Dynasty were also discovered inside the city. Now the shanma city is the provincial historical relic protection site. It consists of Inner Part, Outer Part and trench, and in the east is the steep Mahe River Valley.

雄 揽胜

雄
揽胜
XIONGGUANLANSHENG

雄
揽胜

雄
揽 胜

雄
揽胜
XIONGGUANLANSHENG

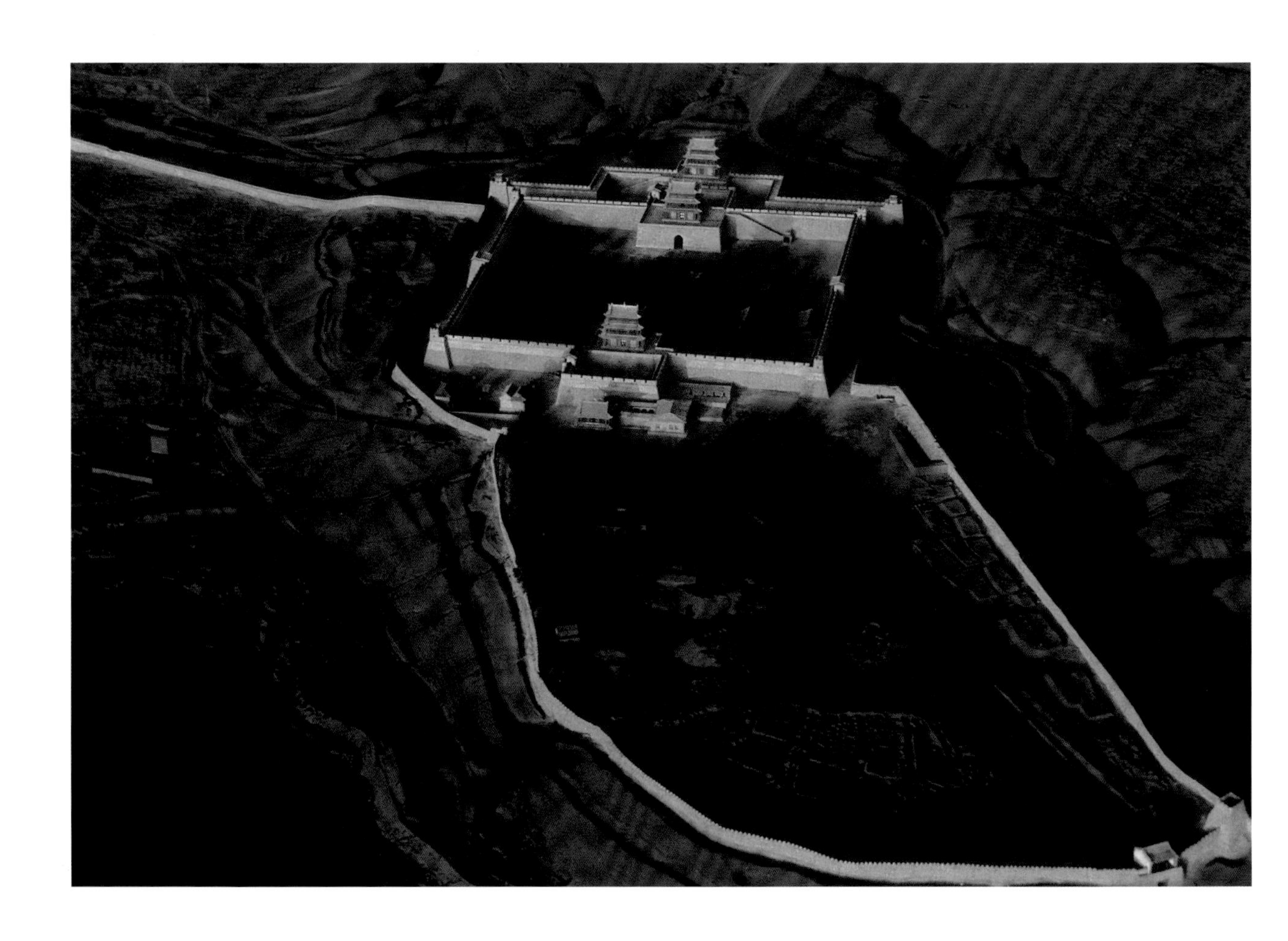

雄
揽胜

雄
揽胜

雄关揽胜

雄
揽胜

雄
揽胜

雄
揽胜

雄 揽胜

嘉峪关长城博物馆

Jiayuguan Great Wall Museum

嘉峪关长城博物馆是我国长城沿线上第一座博物馆，建成于1989年10月。经过10多年的发展，得到了文博界专家学者和广大游客的好评，也引起了党和国家领导人的高度重视。但由于原馆地处市区、距关城较远，不便于参观，1998年，嘉峪关市委、市政府决定将长城博物馆迁至嘉峪关关城下。新馆建成于2003年4月，占地面积4523平方米，建筑面积3599平方米。该馆采用了半地下式的建筑方案，古朴、凝重，藏而不露。上小图为原馆，上图为新馆。

Jiayuguan Great Wall Museum is the first museum along the Great Wall,which had been built in October ,1989.With its development of more than ten years,it received much favorable comment from the specialists and scholars in cultural circles and museology and from the numerous tourists.It also attracted much attention from the Leaders of our Party and our Country. Because the old museum was situated downtown and a little far from the castle,it was inconvenient to visit.In 1998,the Jiayuyuan City Committee and City Government decided to move the museum to the foot of the Jiayu pass.The new museum had been built in April,2003,with a ground area of 4253m^2 and a building area of 3599m^2. With a half underground style,the museum is simple,dignified and goes into hiding.The above picture is the old museum,the above left is the new one.

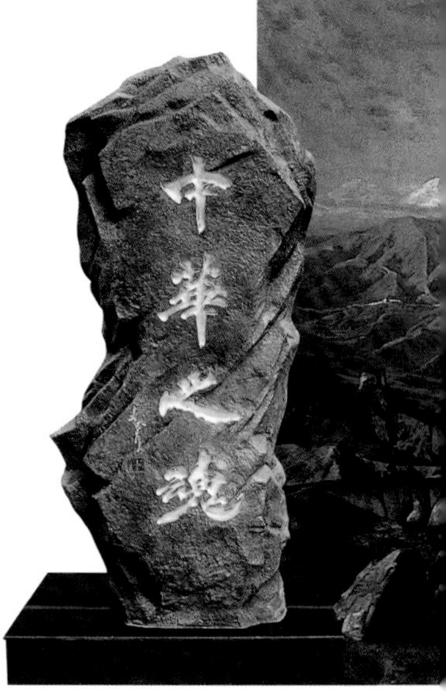

嘉峪关长城博物馆是以展示长城文化、长城历史和长城学研究成果为一体的专题性博物馆。“中华之魂——长城历史文化陈列”共分4个单元，6个展厅，内容丰富，历史详实，可视性强，艺术品味高。

Jiayuguan Great Wall Museum is a subject museum for exhibiting the Great Wall culture,the Great Wall history and the studying achievements of the Great Wall subject.“The lofty Spirit of China —Exhibition of the History and Culture of the Great Wall” consists of four units in six halls with abundant contents,authentic historical materials, good visuality and high artistic level.

大型油画“长城万里图”，以写意和写实相结合的表现手法将中国东部、中部、西部长城的主要景观浓缩于画卷之中。此画长21米，高10.5米，总面积220平方米，是西北目前博物馆中最大的油画。

The huge painting “Ten-Thousand-Mile Picture of the Great Wall” concentrates main spots at the eastern,middle and western parts of the Great Wall with expressing method both realistic and freehand.The painting is 21m long,10.5m high,with on area of 220 square meters.It’s the largest painting in the museums of the Northwest.

超写实雕塑场景——“西出阳关·春风玉门”运用现代高分子材料以超写实雕塑为表现手法，生动地刻画了守关将士“西出阳关”时的依依惜别之情和胡商牵驼，情绪高昂。春风满面的入关之景，再现了当年“西出阳关无故人”、“春风已度玉门关”的真实情景。

Superrealistic Sculpture Sights —“Going west out of the Yang pass,Spring Wind Kissing Yumen”,using the modern high-molecular materials and the expressing method of super-realistic sculptures,exhibit vividly their departing feelings when the generals and soldiers defending the pass“go west out of the Yang Pass”and the sights when the Hu - merchants entering the pass handing their camels,with high spirit and full of joy .This makes relive the then real sights showing “One will has no old friend when one goes west out of the Yang Pass” and “The Spring wind has been arrived at the Yumen Pass”.

博物馆内设有影视厅、学术报告厅、休闲厅、购物厅、资料室、多媒体自动查询系统等附属设施和安防、报警、消防自动监控系统，在省内属领先水平。图为环境优美的休闲厅和影视厅。

In the museum,there are a film and TV hall, a symposium hall,a resting hall,a shopping hall, a reference room,a multimedia auto-requirement system and an auto-supervision system for safety , alarm and fire.This has a high level in the province. The pictures are the resting hall and film and TV hall with beautiful environments.

滑 翔 基 地 Jiayuguan International Gliding Base

嘉峪关国际滑翔基地是1987年国家投资90多万元建设起来的我国第一个可用于国际比赛和接待外国运动员训练之用的滑翔基地。据有关方面多次考察，嘉峪关由于地域开阔、干燥少雨、日照时间长，适应滑翔所需的三种气流，即上升气流（决定飞行距离）、动力气流（决定飞行速度）、波浪气流（决定飞行高度），三种气流兼得，实为世界罕见。在这里，滑翔机每天飞行时间可达10多个小时，每年飞行时间可达6个月。该基地已成为与澳大利亚、南非相媲美的世界三大滑翔场地之一。嘉峪关市曾举办过二届国际滑翔节。

Jiayuguan International Gliding Base was built in 1987 with more than 900 thousand RMB invested by the nation. It is the first one which could be used for international competitions and to meet the foreign athletes.

It has been inspected for many times that because of the wideness, dryness and long time of sun shining, there are all the three kinds of air suitable for gliding. This is rare in the world. Here, glider planes could soar more than 10 hours everyday, 6 months each year.

The base has become one of the largest three bases in the world.

黑 山 石 刻

Stone Inscriptions on the Black Mountain

黑山石刻地处甘肃嘉峪关市西北15公里处的黑山峡谷之中。黑山石刻发现于1972年，在东西走向，长约10多公里的峡谷崖壁上，散布着140多处石刻遗迹。画面最小的0.23米，大的3米多，主要形象有人物、马、牛、羊、狗、骆驼、鹿、虎、蛇、鱼等，主要场面有操练、游牧、狩猎等。笔法流利、气势不凡。据有关专家推测，嘉峪关黑山石刻是战国至秦汉时期的产物。

The stone inscriptions on the Black Mountain are located in the Black Mountain valley, 15 km northwest of Jiayuguan city. They were discovered in 1972. On the valley precipices, there are more than 140 stone inscriptions. The smallest is 0.23m long and the biggest over 3 m. The main images are human beings, horses, oxen, sheep, dogs, camels, deer, tigers, snakes and fish etc. The strokes are smooth and the style imposing.

七 一 冰 川 July First Glacier

七一冰川位于嘉峪关市西南部的祁连山中，距市区约116公里，海拔4300多米。1958年7月1日，中国科学院冰雪研究队第一次发现该冰川，因此命名。

七一冰川是典型的大陆性冰川，面积4平方公里，冰层厚度100—120米，是当今世界上距离城市最近的冰川之一。

七一冰川景观奇特，易于攀登。远远望去，巨大的冰川像一座玲珑剔透的玉雕，横卧于东西两山之间，洁白晶莹。雪峰顶端与蓝天白云相接，冰舌下端与山谷溪水为伴，十分壮观。陡峭的冰崖、直立的冰墙、垂吊的冰帘、千奇百怪的冰钟乳和深不可测的冰缝，向人们展示了无与伦比的冰上美景。目前通达七一冰川的道路已全部修通。

The July 1 Glacier is situated in the Qilain mountains. It was found on July 1, 1956, and so had the name.

The glacier is a typical continental one, with an area of 4 square kilometers, the thickness of the ice layer 100-120 meters, and one of the nearest glaciers from city in the world

Looking from far, the huge glacier, white and icy, is like a dainty and exquisite jade sculpture lying between the eastern and the western mountains. The snowy peaks kiss the blue sky and the white clouds, the ice tongues lick the river water in the valley. The stiff ice cliffs, standing ice walls, hanging ice curtains, various ice stalactites and uncountable ice leaks show you an incomparable ice landscape.

魏晋墓画像砖

Painting Bricks in the Tombs of the Wei Jin Dynasty

嘉峪关魏晋墓群分布于甘肃嘉峪关市区东北部20公里处，在周围约10公里的范围内，经初步踏查，有古墓葬1000余座。已经发掘的13座墓葬，大部分是较大型的砖室墓，多为二室墓和三室墓，形制、结构独特，镶嵌于墓室四壁的画像砖，色调热烈明快，取材于现实生活，是魏晋时代河西走廊政治、经济、军事、文化的真实写照，具有浓厚的生活气息。其中《驿使传报》一幅画面，生动逼真，不仅反映了当时军事上的传报情况，而且对研究我国邮驿史有一定参考价值。

20 kilometers in the northeast of Jiayuguan city, there is a tombs group of the Wei Jin Dynasty which covers about 10 kilometers. The first investigation has found more than a thousand tombs. 13 of them have been excavated. Most of them are made with bricks, each with two or three rooms. The painting bricks inlaid on the four walls have beautiful colors and various contents which cover the politics, economy, military and culture. In them is the vivid painting A Postman Sending A Letter which not only shows the sending situation in the military then but also has a value for studying the post history of our nation. The tombs are called "Underground Art Gallery".

今日嘉峪关 Jiayuguan Today

嘉峪关的高大威武，凝结着历代劳动人民的心血。据确凿的史料记载，自嘉峪关创建以来，曾多次修缮和重修。新中国成立之后，党和政府更加关心嘉峪关的维修和保护。国家地方共筹资3000多万元，对嘉峪关楼进行了三次大规模的重建。使嘉峪关以更加宏伟的气魄，闻名遐迩，显示了中华民族强大的凝聚力。

今日的嘉峪关，西部的苍凉和塞北的绿洲，景观迥异；大漠孤烟，长河落日，祁连雪峰，构成了古老长城文化的超凡意境；红柳白杨，水磨清泉，驿站民居又组成了绿洲文化的另一道风景线。景区占地面积2万平米，分关城游览区、文化展示区、九眼泉湖、休闲度假区、仿古集市、儿童村、民俗村、西部植物园、西部风情园，服务设施和基础设施一应俱全，整个景区与嘉峪关关城，巧妙地融合为一体，风景秀丽，地域特色鲜明，丰富了长城文化的内涵，吸引了大量的游客。

博 物 馆

Jiayu Pass, being high and mighty, is the contribution from all generations of the people. After the foundation of the new China, the Party and the government pay more attentions to the repair and the protection for the Jiayu Pass. More than 30 millions of RMB was raised by the local and the country's governments, and the castle was rebuilt in a large scale for three times. So, the Jiayu Pass, with it's more magnificent spirit, is famous all over the world. This exhibits the strong cohesion of the Chinese nation.

In today's Jiayu Pass, the Cultural Touring Zone of the Jiayuguan Great Wall has been built. The solitary smoke twisting over the desert, the bending sun behind the long river, the snowy peaks of the Qilian Mountains, all this give you a feeling beyond this world. The red willows and white poplars, water mills and clear springs, the post and citizens' houses make up another landscape of the oasis culture. The service and base facilities are all complete. The whole zone combines itself with the Jiayuguan castle as a whole ingeniously. The beautiful landscapes, the clear local characters, richen the Great Wall culture, attract a great lot of tourists.

龙泉山庄

泰和山庄

石雕群

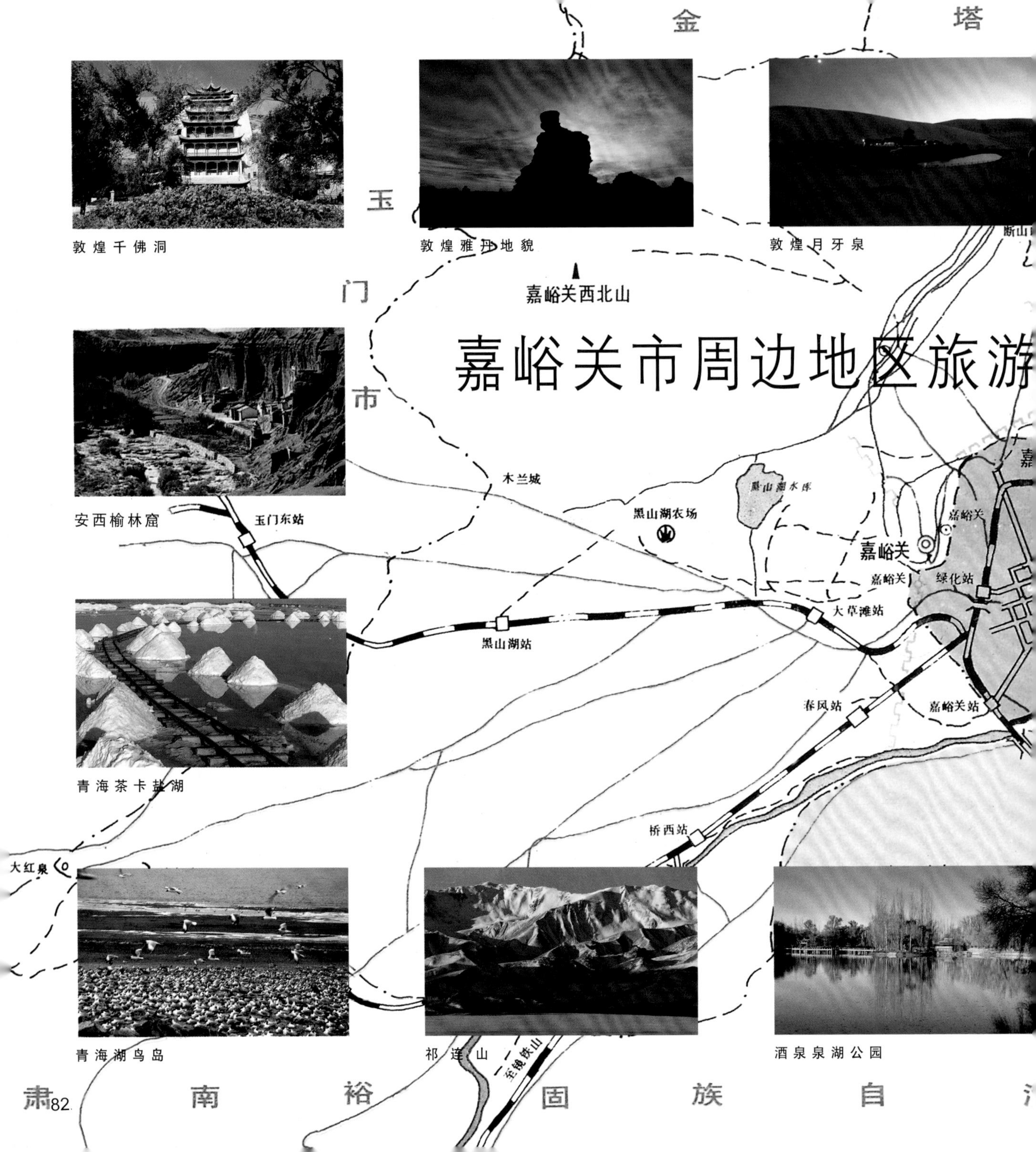
嘉峪关市周边地区旅游
金
塔
玉
门
市
嘉峪关西北山
断山
木兰城
黑山湖水库
黑山湖农场
玉门东站
嘉峪关
嘉峪关
嘉峪关
绿化站
大草滩站
黑山湖站
春风站
嘉峪关站
桥西站
大红泉
至镜铁山
敦煌千佛洞
敦煌雅丹地貌
敦煌月牙泉
安西榆林窟
青海茶卡盐湖
青海湖鸟岛
祁连山
酒泉泉湖公园
肃
南
裕
固
族
自

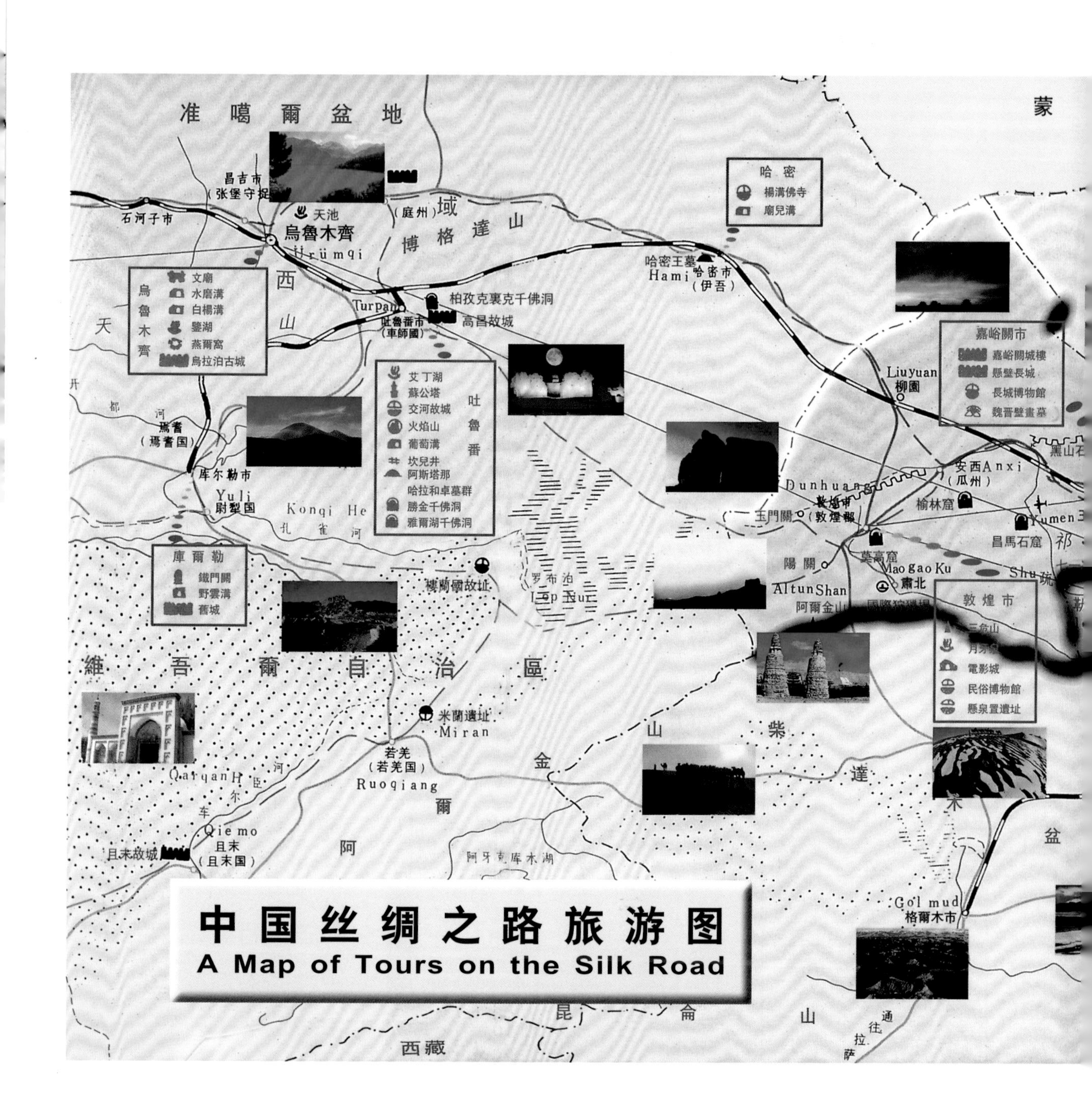
中国丝绸之路旅游图
A Map of Tours on the Silk Road
准噶爾盆地
昌吉市
(张堡守捉)
石河子市
天池
烏魯木齊
Urümqi
(庭州)
博格達山
哈密
楊溝佛寺
廟兒溝
哈密王墓
Hami
哈密市
(伊吾)
烏魯木齊
文廟
水磨溝
白楊溝
鹽湖
燕爾窩
烏拉泊古城
西山
天山
Turpan
吐魯番市
(車師國)
柏孜克裏克千佛洞
高昌故城
艾丁湖
蘇公塔
交河故城
火焰山
葡萄溝
坎兒井
阿斯塔那
哈拉和卓墓群
勝金千佛洞
雅爾湖千佛洞
吐魯番
嘉峪關市
嘉峪關城樓
懸壁長城
長城博物館
魏晉壁畫墓
Liuyuan
柳園
焉耆
(焉耆国)
库尔勒市
Yuli
尉犁国
Konqi He
孔雀河
庫爾勒
鐵門關
野雲溝
舊城
樓蘭國故址
罗布泊
Lop Nur
安西Anxi
(瓜州)
Dunhuang
榆林窟
玉門關
敦煌市
(敦煌郡)
昌馬石窟
Yumen
陽關
莫高窟
Mao gao Ku
AltunShan
阿爾金山
肅北
敦煌市
電影城
民俗博物館
懸泉置遺址
維吾爾自治區
米蘭遺址
Miran
若羌
(若羌国)
Ruoqiang
QarqanHe
Qiemo
且末
(且末国)
且末故城
阿尔金山
阿牙克库木湖
柴達木盆
Golmud
格爾木市
昆侖山
西藏
通往拉萨
蒙

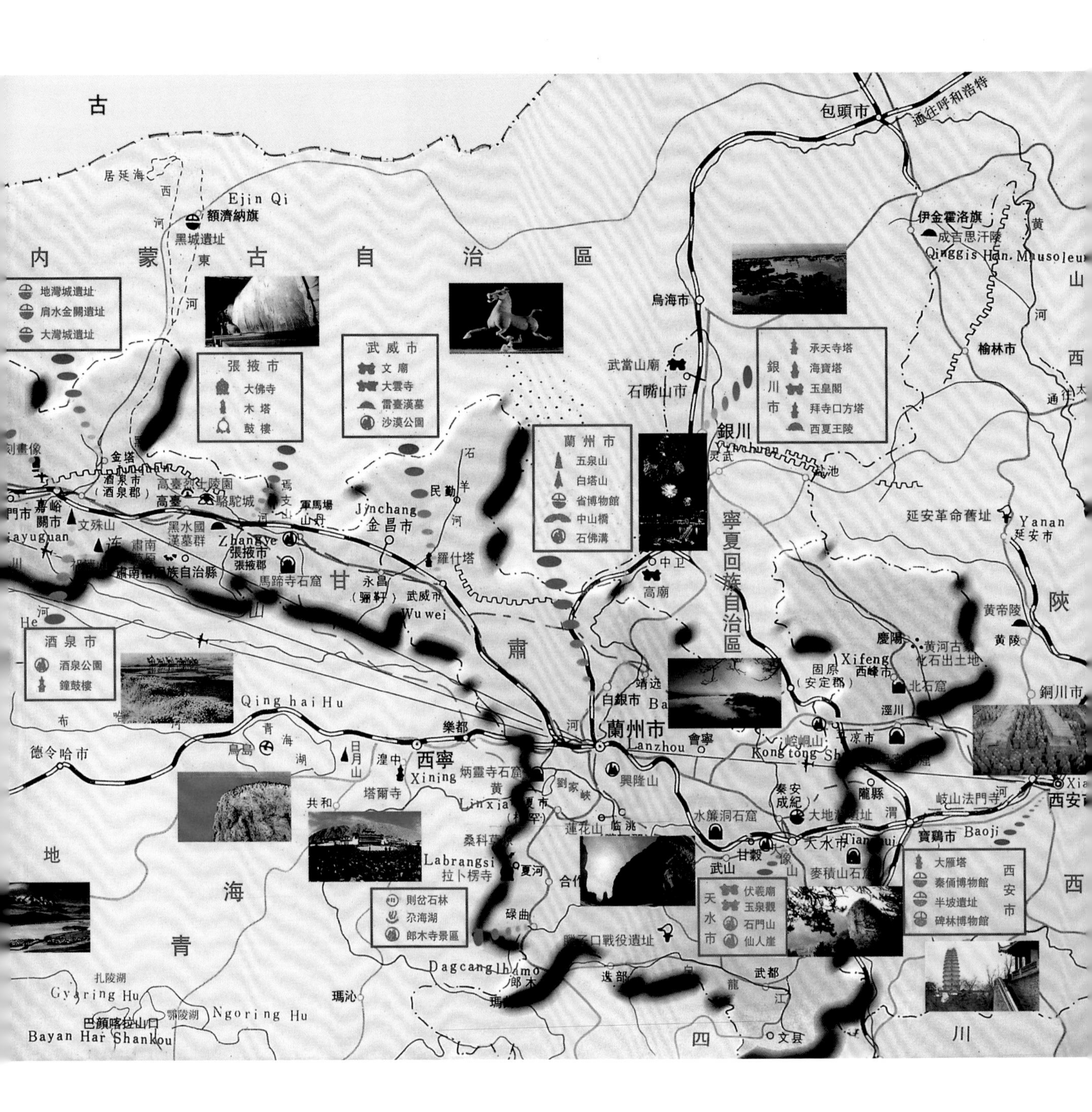

古
包頭市
通往呼和浩特
居延海
Ejin Qi
額濟納旗
黑城遺址
內
蒙
古
自
治
區
伊金霍洛旗
成吉思汗陵
Qinggis Han Mausoleum
地灣城遺址
肩水金關遺址
大灣城遺址
烏海市
張掖市
大佛寺
木塔
鼓樓
武威市
文廟
大雲寺
雷臺漢墓
沙漠公園
承天寺塔
海寶塔
玉皇閣
拜寺口方塔
西夏王陵
銀川市
榆林市
武當山廟
石嘴山市
蘭州市
五泉山
白塔山
省博物館
中山橋
石佛溝
銀川
Yinchuan
靈武
鹽池
金塔
酒泉市
(酒泉郡)
高臺烈士陵園
高臺
駱駝城
軍馬場
山丹
Jinchang
金昌市
民勤
嘉峪關市
文殊山
Jiayuguan
黑水國漢墓群
Zhangye
張掖市
張掖郡
肅南裕固族自治縣
馬蹄寺石窟
羅什塔
永昌
(驪靬)
武威市
Wuwei
甘
肅
中卫
高廟
寧
夏
回
族
自
治
區
延安革命舊址
Yanan
延安市
黃帝陵
陝
慶陽
黃河古象化石出土地
Xifeng
西峰市
北石窟
固原
(安定郡)
酒泉市
酒泉公園
鐘鼓樓
Qing hai Hu
德令哈市
鳥島
青海湖
樂都
日月山
湟中
西寧
Xining
塔爾寺
共和
炳靈寺石窟
劉家峽
白銀市
靖远
蘭州市
Lanzhou
會寧
崆峒山
Kong tong Shan
平涼市
涇川
銅川市
興隆山
臨夏市
Linxia
蓮花山
臨洮
秦安
成紀
大地灣遺址
水簾洞石窟
隴縣
岐山法門寺
寶鷄市
Baoji
西安市
甘穀
天水市
麥積山石窟
武山
桑科草原
Labrangsi
拉卜楞寺
夏河
合作
大雁塔
秦俑博物館
半坡遺址
碑林博物館
西安市
則岔石林
尕海湖
郎木寺景區
伏羲廟
玉泉觀
石門山
仙人崖
天水市
碌曲
臘子口戰役遺址
地
海
青
扎陵湖
Gyaring Hu
鄂陵湖
Ngoring Hu
巴顏喀拉山口
Bayan Har Shankou
瑪沁
Dagcanglhamo
郎木寺
迭部
武都
白龍江
文县
四
川
西

多少疲倦的目光
流入空茫的岁月
多少岁月的霜雪
刻入无言的砖石

当历史打开一扇门
风卷残云之后
只剩下这时间的记忆……

图书在版编目（CIP）数据

天下雄关／王金摄影，胡杨撰文．—兰州：甘肃人民美术出版社，2003

ISBN 7-80588-468-4

Ⅰ．天...　Ⅱ．①王...②胡...　Ⅲ．关隘，嘉峪关—简介—汉、英　Ⅳ．K928.77

中国版本图书馆CIP数据核字（2003）第028917号

责任编辑：罗如琪
装帧设计：邵金昌
英文翻译：石天文
英文校译：高松山

天下雄关

王金　摄影　胡杨　撰文
甘肃人民美术出版社出版发行
（730000 兰州市滨河东路296号）
深圳华新彩印制版有限公司印刷
开本850毫米×1168毫米　1/24　印张4　字数20千
2005年4月第3版　2005年4月第3次印刷
印数：1-5000

ISBN 7-80588-468-4　定价：30.00元